THE ORIGIN OF EVIL
Biblical Truths Hidden in Plain Sight

Dr. Yeral E. Ogando

Dedication

This book is dedicated to all those who seek the Truth in Yahuah, and to those whom Yahuah Elohíym has already opened their eyes and understanding.

May Yahuah grant you wisdom and discernment as you read these pages, created with the purpose of bringing clarity to the people of Yahuah in all nations.

This book is not for the blind nor for the blind guides, who will never understand or see the truth, even when it stands before their faces.

For, in the end, this book does not belong to the nefilim bloodline, but to the pure spiritual bloodline of Yahuah, manifested in Yahusha Ha Mashíyach.

And for us, those who serve Yahuah:

We have not been called to believe without investigation, prayer, and discernment, but to believe after examining all the sources— within and outside of this book—and only after praying, to accept what the ruach of Yahuah confirms as true.

It is fine if you do not agree with everything expressed here; I understand that some will need years to comprehend it, while others already possess a seed of knowledge that comes from Yahuah.

This work is dedicated to those called by Yahuah Elohíym and redeemed by Yahusha Ha Mashíyach.

"Examine all things; hold fast to what is good."
I Thessalonikéfs (I Thessalonians) 5:21

THE ORIGIN OF EVIL
Biblical Truths Hidden in Plain Sight

A chronological reconstruction of the origin, expansion, and destiny of evil according to the restored Scriptures. Dismantling the Lies of the Enemy.

TABLE OF CONTENTS

Introduction

From the beginning of creation, the purpose of Yahuah was to manifest His light, His truth, and His righteousness throughout all creation. However, from the very first days of humankind, the enemy sowed deception. Thus began the untold history of evil — a story that has been distorted, concealed, and reinterpreted by men, fallen angels, and the kingdoms of darkness that seek to twist the revealed truth.

From the beginning of creation, the purpose of Yahuah was to manifest His light, His truth, and His righteousness throughout all creation.

However, from the very first days of humankind, the enemy sowed deception. Thus began the untold history of evil — a story that has been distorted, concealed, and reinterpreted by men, fallen angels, and the kingdoms of darkness that seek to twist the revealed truth.

In the Yarden (Garden of Eden), Gadreel—not the adversary commonly described by modern religion—was the one who seduced Chawwâh (Eve) and led her into sin.

"And the Nâchâsh said to the woman: You will not surely die..." (Bereshith / Genesis 3:4).

From that moment on, humanity became trapped in a web of spiritual corruption that spread throughout the ages.

The Watcher Angels (Nephîyl), mentioned in Chănôk (Enoch) and confirmed in the Scriptures, descended with the purpose of instructing humanity, but once they experienced human form, their purpose changed—to beget offspring.

These beings were seduced, deceived, and led into rebellion against the command of Yahuah.

From their union with the daughters of men were born the Nephilim—hybrid creatures without the ruaḥ (breath) of Yahuah, entirely inclined toward evil.

"There were Nephîyl in the earth in those days, and also afterward, when the sons of ĚLÔHÎYM came in to the daughters of men, and they bore children to them." (Bereshith 6:4)

From their existence came forth the demons—restless spirits wandering in search of bodies to possess, for they belong neither to heaven nor to the creation of Yahuah.

The Flood was not merely a physical catastrophe but a spiritual purification.

Yahuah preserved eight souls—Noaḥ, his wife, his three sons, and their wives—to guard the holy seed, the only one that retained His ruaḥ.

"And, behold, I, even I, do bring a flood of waters upon the earth, to destroy all flesh, wherein is the breath of life, from under heaven; and everything that is in the earth shall die." (Bereshith 6:17)

Yet even after the flood, a nefilim remnant survived and settled in the regions of Ararat (arrat) and Babel.

It was in the days of Qeynan (Cainan), a descendant of Noaḥ (Noah), that wickedness once again flourished.

Qeynan found the ancient teachings of the Watchers, copied them, and taught them to men—reintroducing magic, idolatry, witchcraft, and forbidden sciences.

From Babel, the center of rebellion, arose the tower, symbol of pride and confusion.

"And YAHUAH came down to see the city and the tower, which the children of men built... and there confound their language." (Bereshith 11:5–9)

Thus the Watchers and their remnant were scattered, later dominating the neighboring nations—including Sodom and Gomorrah, cities corrupted by the nefilim seed.

From this lineage came the Chasmoniym, fathers of the Philistines, and later the Pharisees, Sadducees, and Essenes, who inherited the same nefilim blood.

They usurped the temple, corrupted the priesthood, and rose against Yahusha Ha Mashíyach, the Son of Elyôn.

"You are of your father the diabolos, and the lusts of your father you will do." (Yôchânân / John 8:44)

In them the prophecy was fulfilled—the sons of the Nâchâsh persecuting the Son of Man.

Maśṭêmâh, prince of demons, is not a wandering spirit, but a physical being—an angel with a body—who operates as head of the nefilim remnant.

From Mitsrayim (Egypt) to Rome, his dominion has extended under different forms, concealed within religions, philosophies, and human empires.

Over time, Babel was reincarnated in the Roman Empire, under Constantine, who blended the teachings of the nefilim with the name of the true Êlôhîym, creating a false universal religion.

In this way, Babel devoured the nations once again through its lies, corrupting the sacred name of Yahuah and replacing it with idols and doctrines of men.

This work reveals that evil did not originate from the human flesh created by Yahuah, but from the mixture between the celestial and the terrestrial.

And just as its origin was a forbidden union, its end will be a final separation—the judgment of Yahuah upon the kingdoms of darkness.

Chapter 1
The Creation and the First Fall
(The Beginning of Order... and of Chaos)

1.1 Creation of All Spirits on the First Day of Creation

(The Beginning of the Invisible World and the Eternal Nature of Spiritual Beings)

The angels received the gift of eternity; therefore, as they are eternal, they do not procreate nor reproduce.

Chănôk (Enoch) – Chapter 15: Verses 6–7
"As for you, you were first spiritual, living an eternal life,
immortal through all the generations of the world; therefore,
wives have not been appointed to you, for the dwelling of the
spirits of the shâmayim is in the shâmayim."

Yôbêl (Jubilees) – Chapter 2: Verses 2–3
"For on the first day He created the shâmayim above, the earth,
the waters, and all the spirits that serve Him: the angels of the
presence, the angels of sanctification, the angels of the spirit of
fire, the angels of the spirit of the winds, the angels of the spirit of
the clouds, of darkness, of snow, of hail, and of frost, the angels
of the voices, of thunder and lightning, the angels of the spirits of
cold and heat, of winter, spring, autumn, and summer, and all
the spirits of His creatures that are in the shâmayim and on the
earth. He created the abysses, the darkness, the evening and the
night, and the light, the dawn, and the day— all these things He
prepared in the knowledge of His heart. And then we saw His
works and praised Him and gloried in His presence for all His
works, for seven great works He created on the first day."

The seven great works created on the first day:

1. Shâmayim

2. Waters

3. Angels

4. Spirit of man

5. Abysses

6. Darkness

7. Light

Contrary to what we have been told or taught, the Scriptures teach that all the spirits of mankind were also created on the first day of creation.

That means every human being who has not yet taken on flesh and blood—who has not yet been born—was, in reality, created from the very first day of creation.

Yirmeyâhû (Jeremiah) – Chapter 1: Verse 5
"Before I formed you in the belly I knew you; and before you came forth out of the womb I sanctified you, and I ordained you a prophet unto the nations."

Tehîllîm (Psalms) – Chapter 139: Verse 13
"For you have possessed my reins: you have covered me in my mother's womb."

As we see in these verses, the angels—also created on the first day of creation—received the gift of eternal life. Their nature, therefore, is not one of reproduction; that is why all angels are masculine. There is no such thing as a female angel—this concept is unbiblical.

All are masculine because the ability to procreate or reproduce was not assigned to them, but rather eternity in the heavens. The angels were created as servants of Yahuah's most precious creation—Man. The angels were created to serve us, not for us to serve the angels.

1.2 Creation of Humans on the Sixth Day

(The Gift of Procreation and the Connection with the ruach of Yahuah)

Humans, as ephemeral and mortal beings, received the unique gift of procreation so that they would not perish from the earth, but continue to multiply. This great gift was given only to mankind.

Yôbêl (Jubilees) – Chapter 2: Verses 14–15
"And after all this he created man, a man and a woman he created them, and gave him dominion over all that is upon the earth, and in the seas, and over everything that flies, and over beasts and over cattle, and over everything that moves on the earth, and over the whole earth, and over all this he gave him dominion. And these four kinds he created on the sixth day. And there were altogether two and twenty kinds."

1. Land animals

2. Cattle

3. Everything that moves on the earth

4. Man

Yahuah worked with great care in His creation, establishing all that was necessary for His greatest work to enjoy and live with Him forever.

As His final masterpiece, on the sixth day He created man, His magnificent creation. Everything He had created from the first day until that moment on the sixth day was the preparation of the environment to bring man into life—to enjoy the paradise Yahuah had made.

Chănôk (Enoch) – Chapter 15: Verse 5
"Therefore I have given them women also that they might impregnate them, and beget children by them, that thus nothing might be wanting to them on earth."

Since man did not receive the immortality of the angels, he was given a unique and special gift—the ability to beget and procreate children on the earth, ensuring that nothing would be lacking in the creation of Yahuah.

This faculty of bearing children and descendants is the most precious gift of our existence—envied and coveted by some of the angels.

Let us remember that all the spirits of men were created on the first day of creation, but only on the sixth day did that spirit receive a body and become a living human being.

This is why in the text of Berēshīth (Genesis) it is explained that male and female were created (on the first day), but only on the sixth day did man become a living being.

1.3 Chawwâh in the Garden

(The Seduction by Gadreel (Gadriel) and the Entrance of Deception into Eden)

Chawwâh, in the Garden, was seduced by Gadriel and fell into temptation.

The woman succumbed to the suggestion of the angel Gadriel—not of a serpent—and the woman, in turn, shared with the man the fruit of that temptation.

Chănôk (Enoch) – Chapter 69: Verse 6 "And the third was named Gadreel... and he led astray Chawwâh..."

As we see, it was an angel—not a reptile. This same angel later joined the fallen Watchers.

Yôbêl (Jubilees) – Chapter 3: Verses 17–19 "
And after the completion of the seven years, which he had completed there, seven years exactly, and in the second month, on the seventeenth day of the month, the Nâchâsh came and approached the woman, and the Nâchâsh said to the woman, has Êlôhîym commanded you, saying, you shall not eat of every tree of the garden? And she said to it, of all the fruit of the trees of the garden Êlôhîym has said unto us, eat; but of the fruit of the tree which is in the midst of the garden Êlôhîym has said unto us, shall not eat thereof, neither shall you touch it, lest you die. And the Nâchâsh said unto the woman, you shall not surely die: For Êlôhîym does know that on the day you shall eat thereof, your eyes will be opened, and you will be as gods, and you will know good and evil."

Adam and Chawwâh dwelt in the garden for seven years, cultivating it and being cared for by Yahuah Êlôhîym.

The Nâchâsh presented a subtle question to the woman, who fell into the trap and repeated what she knew—they had only one prohibition, one specific tree.

If we look closely, the only lie spoken by the Nâchâsh was when he said, "You will not die."

The woman fell into the trap—not by force but by suggestion—and sinned.

Immediately her eyes were opened, and she knew evil, for she already knew good.

The fruit represented the knowledge of evil—or rather, disobedience to everything that is good or lawful.

Even after this sin that marked the course of all creation—born from the union of the woman and the angel Nâchâsh—there was nothing inherently evil in the creation of Élôhîym.

The consequences of disobedience brought corruption, for everything He created was very good.

1.4 Gadreel or Gadriel – Before the Watchers

(The True Adversary Who Introduced Death and Error)

Chănôk (Enoch) – Chapter 69: Verse 6
"And the third was named Gadreel: He it is who showed the children of men all the blows of death, and he led astray Chawwâh, and showed the weapons of death to the sons of men, the shield and the coat of mail, and the sword for battle, and all the weapons of death to the children of men."

Gadreel was never part of the sin of the Watchers and was never imprisoned. He is the one we know as the adversary.

He later took advantage of the sin of the Watchers—those angels who corrupted themselves with women—to transmit forbidden teachings to humanity and to the descendants of the Nephilim.

His first appearance was in the Garden of Eden at the beginning of creation, crafting the first deception, and for that act he was cursed by Yahuah.

1.5 Expulsion from Paradise

(The Consequence of Disobedience)

M an was expelled from Paradise—the Garden of Eden—for his transgression, and the entrance to Paradise was guarded and hidden so that humans could not find it.

Berēshīth (Genesis) – Chapter 3: Verses 22–24
"And YAHUAH ĔLÔHÎYM said, Behold, Âdâm is become as one of us, to know good and evil: and now, lest he put forth his hand, and take also of the tree of life, and eat, and live forever: Therefore YAHUAH ĔLÔHÎYM sent him forth from the garden of Eden, to till the ground from whence he was taken. So he drove out the man; and he placed at the east of the garden of Eden Kerûb, and a flaming sword which turned every way, to keep the way of the tree of life."

1.6 The First Murder in Humanity

(Qayin Against Hebel: The Birth of Bloodshed)

Q ayin, driven by jealousy and envy, became the first murderer of the human race.

However, even after this event, evil itself had not yet prevailed upon the earth.

Yôbêl (Jubilees) – Chapter 4: Verse 2
"And in the first year of the third jubilee, Qayin slew Hebel because Êlôhîym accepted the sacrifice of Hebel, and did not accept the offering of Qayin."

Berēshīth (Genesis) – Chapter 4: Verses 3–4
"And in process of time it came to pass, that Qayin brought of the

fruit of the ground an offering unto YAHUAH. And Hebel, he also brought of the firstlings of his flock and of the fat thereof. And YAHUAH had respect unto Hebel and to his offering"

- Min perîy: Qayin offered part of his fruit or harvest.

- Min bekôrâh: Hebel offered the best—the firstborn.

This is the whole matter—there is no need to complicate it or overanalyze.

Qayin did not give the best, while Hebel did; therefore, Yahuah accepted the best.

Qayin, filled with jealousy, became the first murderer of humanity.

With this first murder, Hebel became the first innocent martyr to lose his life for truth—by giving the best to Yahuah.

1.7 After the First Murder

(A Stage without Demons or Fallen Watchers)

Even after all this, there was not yet the kind of evil that would later overwhelm creation.

There existed the knowledge of evil, and therefore, every human being born from the creation of Yahuah was born with the understanding of what is good and what is evil.

By yielding to emotion, mankind had the ability to perform evil; however, in this stage of humanity, there were still no demons, no fallen Watchers, no diseases, nor the calamities that would come later.

1.8 The First Invocation of the Name of Yahuah

After the times of Adam, came the times of Seth, and then the times of Enosh—from the lineage of Seth (not Enosh from the lineage of Qayin).

Then, for the first time on earth, the name of Êlôhîym was invoked.

Berēshîṯh (Genesis) – Chapter 4: Verse 26
"And to Shêth, to him also there was born a son; and he called his name Ĕnôsh: then began men to call upon the name of YAHUAH."

Let us pay close attention not to confuse Enosh of the lineage of Sheth with Enosh of the lineage of Qayin.

It was only when, from the descendants of Sheth, Enosh was born that humans began for the first time to invoke the name of Yahuah— not before, and not from the descendants of Qayin.

The generations passed—from Qayin, through Mahalalel—until reaching the generation of Yarad.

Capítulo 2
The Rebellion of the Watchers and the Corruption of the Earth

(When the sons of heaven descended and sowed wickedness among men.)

2.1 The Watcher Angels

(The celestial emissaries sent to instruct mankind)

The Watcher Angels were sent in the days of Yârad as heavenly ambassadors to teach the laws of Êlôhîym to humanity.

Yôbêl (Jubilees) 4:15
"And in the second week of the tenth jubilee Mahălalêl took unto him to woman Dıynâh, the daughter of Barâkîêl, the daughter of his father's brother, and she bare him a son in the third week in the sixth year, and he called his name Yârad, for in his days the angels of Yahuah descended on the earth, those who are named the Watchers, that they should instruct the children of men, and that they should do judgment and uprightness on the earth."

The true purpose for which Yahuah sent the Watcher angels to the earth was to teach His laws that righteousness and justice might prevail among men. However, when they took on human form, they began to experience the same needs as the creation of Êlôhîym—mankind itself. They were tempted and influenced by other angels; the Watchers too were lured and fell into temptation. There were angels behind them persuading them to commit the one act they were absolutely forbidden to do—to beget offspring or have descendants.

Chănôk (Enoch) 69:4–5
*"The name of the first Yeqon: That is, the one who led astray all
the sons of Êlôhîym, and brought them down to the earth, and
led them astray through the daughters of men. And the second
was named Asbeel: He imparted to the qâdôsh sons of Êlôhîym
evil counsel, and led them astray so that they defiled their bodies
with the daughters of men."*

As we can see from these verses, the main leaders who incited
corruption—deceiving the Watchers—were Yeqon and Asbeel.
These two chief angels, though scarcely mentioned elsewhere,
were the masterminds behind the seduction that caused the
Watchers to defile themselves with women. The Watcher Angels
themselves were deceived into sin. But why?

Chănôk (Enoch) 6:6
*"And they were in all two hundred; who descended in the days
of Yârad on the summit of Mount Chermôn, and they called it
Mount Chermôn, because they had sworn and bound themselves
by mutual spoken curse upon it."*

It was in the days of Yârad that the Watcher Angels descended to
the earth, and at that time, human corruption had not yet begun.

2.2 The Covenant of Mount Hermon

(The oath of rebellion and the creation of the Nephilim)

When the Watcher Angels came to earth to teach the
laws of Êlôhîym, they took on human form. Thus their
bodies began to experience the same desires as those of
mankind.

However, the only prohibition—the one thing forbidden to them—
was to beget or procreate, for they are eternal beings.

Yet, as they lived among humans and beheld the beauty of women, being persuaded to experience what was unnatural for them, they decided among themselves—about two hundred in total—to make a solemn oath on Mount Hermon to carry out this great sin.

They knew perfectly well that it was a grave transgression; yet, to ensure that none would back out, they sealed their pact with a mutual curse, thereby confirming their own doom.

They desired to have offspring. Eternity was not enough for them—they wanted to procreate.

This sealed not only the fate of that cursed covenant but also the fate of the women who agreed to become companions to the angels.

Chănôk (Enoch) 6:3–6

"And Semyaza, who was their leader, said unto them: I fear you will not indeed agree to do this deed, and I alone shall have to pay the penalty of a great sin. And they all answered him and said: Let us all swear an oath, and all bind ourselves by mutual spoken curse not to abandon this plan but to do this thing. Then they all swore together and bound themselves by mutual spoken curse upon it. And they were in all two hundred; who descended in the days of Yârad on the summit of Mount Chermôn, and they called it Mount Chermôn, because they had sworn and bound themselves by mutual spoken curse upon it."

They fully understood the magnitude of their sin and that punishment awaited them if they carried out their plans. Yet, to guarantee that no one would retreat, they decided to make an oath. To us humans, that might sound simple, for we often swear and fail to keep our word. But angels know that an oath is something unbreakable—it must be fulfilled, no matter the cost. Thus, they sealed their plan with a mutual curse, ensuring there was no turning back.

And if someone still wonders why—what was the purpose of all this? It is simple: I have said it many times. Angels cannot beget or procreate—they cannot have children, lineage, or descendants. This ability belongs to mankind alone. The goal of the Watcher Angels was to create a lineage for themselves, to experience the unique gift given to man—the power to unite with a woman and bring forth life.

2.3 The Beginning of Evil and Corruption

(The birth of hybrids and the total corruption of humanity)

Only man has the ability to beget and bring forth life, and only man can bring forth a living being who is born with that connection or spirit that binds them to Êlôhîym. Just as Êlôhîym breathed his spirit into man at creation, man, when he begets, shares that spirit with the new creature—thus passing on that divine bond.

However, angels, not possessing that creative spirit—for they were not made to procreate—cannot impart their spirit to any being.

They cannot beget anyone bearing the spirit of Êlôhîym.

Chănôk (Enoch) 7:1–6
"And all the others together with them took unto themselves women, and each chose for himself one, and they began to go in unto them and to defile themselves with them, and they taught them charms and enchantments, and the cutting of roots, and made them acquainted with plants. And they became pregnant, and they bare great nephîyl, whose height was three thousand ells: Who consumed all the acquisitions of men. And when men could no longer sustain them, The nephîyl turned against them and devoured mankind. And they began to sin against birds, and beasts, and reptiles, and fish, and to devour one another's flesh, and drink the blood. Then the earth laid accusation against the lawless ones."

The nephîyl, known to us as the Nephilim, are remembered mainly as the giants, for they became the most infamous. They spread rapidly, consuming all the resources of mankind. When men could no longer sustain them, the Nephilim turned to devour (literally eat) humans and every living creature. Likewise, they began to sin—mixing with or corrupting—birds (hybrid bird species), beasts (centaurs...), reptiles, and fish. And when there was nothing left to corrupt, they fought and devoured one another. To make matters worse, they drank the blood of every living thing—the origin of the forbidden practice of drinking or consuming blood.

They murdered and destroyed all of creation, and the blood of the innocent cried out before Yahuah.

When women bore the offspring of the Watcher Angels, the result was hybrid creatures—part human (from the women's genetic line) and part angelic (from the angels' essence).

But since angels do not carry the human seed capable of transmitting the spirit of Êlôhîym, the children born from the union of women and the Watchers were entirely corrupt and evil.

Chănôk (Enoch) 106:17
"And they shall produce on the earth nephîyl not according to the spirit, but according to the flesh, and there shall be a great punishment on the earth, and the earth shall be cleansed from all impurity."

They lacked that "spiritual chip" that connects man with Yahuah; they were not spiritual beings capable of communion with anything good. They were purely carnal and depraved.

Bârûk (Baruch) 3:27–28
"Yahuah did not choose those, neither he gave the way of knowledge unto them: But they were destroyed, because they had no wisdom, and perished through their own foolishness."

Chănôk (Enoch) 15:8–12
"And now, the nephîyl, who are produced from the spirits and
flesh, shall be called evil spirits upon the earth, and on the earth
shall be their dwelling. Evil spirits have proceeded from their
bodies; because they are born from men and from the qâdôsh
Watchers is their beginning and primal origin; they shall be evil
spirits on earth, and evil spirits shall they be called. As for the
spirits of shâmayim, in shâmayim shall be their dwelling, but as
for the spirits of the earth which were born upon the earth, on
the earth shall be their dwelling. And the spirits of the nephîyl
afflict, oppress, destroy, attack, do battle, and work destruction on
the earth, and cause trouble: They take no food, but nevertheless
hunger and thirst, and cause offences. And these spirits shall rise
up against the children of men and against the women, because
they have proceeded from them."

Giants were born—but not only giants. There were also dwarfs,
elves, centaurs—all those hybrid beings we are told belong to
mythology or science fiction.

But they were not fiction; they were real beings that existed—
deformed in every way and utterly evil.

Yôbêl (Jubilees) 7:22
"And they begat sons the Nâphîdîm, and they were all unlike,
and they devoured one another: and the Nephîyl slew the Nâphîl,
and the Nâphîl slew the Elyô, and the Elyô mankind, and one
man another."

2.4 Hybrid Beings in the Mythologies of the World

This section compares the principal hybrid beings of the world's mythologies, showing their cultural origin, description, symbolic meaning, and possible parallels with the Nephilim or Watchers mentioned in Scripture.

• *Hebrew / Apocryphal Tradition – Nefelîm / Gibborim*

Giants, sons of the "sons of Êlôhîym" and human women. Symbol of the corruption of creation and tyrannical power. Direct parallel — origin of hybrid lineage.

• *Mesopotamian – Apkallu (Watchers / Abgal)*

Part human, part fish or bird. They taught forbidden knowledge and were punished. Fallen beings similar to the Watchers of Chǎnôk.

• *Mesopotamian – Lamasu / Shedu*

Human head, body of bull or winged lion. Guardians of temples and gates. Remnants of the "mighty" hybrids.

• *Egyptian – Anubis*

Human body, jackal head. Guardian of the dead. Animal-human hybrid linked to death.

• *Egyptian – Horus*

Human body, falcon head. God of the sky, son of Isis and Osiris. Symbol of divine-human mixture.

• *Egyptian – Thoth*

Human body, ibis head. God of wisdom and writing. Echo of fallen angels who taught forbidden arts.

• *Greek – Centaur*

Half man, half horse. Conflict between instinct and intellect. Hybrid corruption of creation.

- *Greek – Minotaur*

Man's body, bull's head. Result of an unnatural union. Direct allegory of forbidden hybrid birth.

- *Greek – Satyr / Faun*

Half man, half goat. Lust, music, and chaos. Parallel to the sexual corruption of the Watchers.

- *Greek – Chimera*

Lion, goat, and serpent combined. Monster of chaos. Symbol of unnatural hybrid life.

- *Greek – Sirens*

Women with bodies of fish or birds. Seductive and deceptive. Hybrid spirits of deception.

- *Greek / Egyptian – Sphinx*

Human head, lion's body. Guardian of secrets and portals. Hybrid guardian of forbidden knowledge.

- *Norse / Germanic – Werewolves / Berserkers*

Human-animal transformation. Rage and loss of control. Nephilim possession or corruption.

- *Norse – Jötnar (Giants)*

Descendants of gods and giants. Chaos and rebellion against divine order. Northern echo of the Nefelîm.

- *Hindu / Vedic – Narasimha*

Half lion, half man. Divine incarnation of justice. Divine version of a redemptive hybrid.

- *Hindu / Vedic – Garuda*

Half man, half eagle. Mount of Vishnu, enemy of serpents.

Remnant of divine animal fusion.

- *Hindu / Vedic – Kinnara / Gandharva*

Celestial beings with bird or horse forms. Divine musicians. Parallels to "sons of heaven."

- *Hindu / Vedic – Makara*

Aquatic hybrid beast. Vehicle of water deities. Symbol of mixing between realms.

- *Chinese / East Asian – Dragon Kings*

Human-dragon forms. Guardians of seas and weather. Echo of fallen beings ruling nature.

- *Japanese – Tengu*

Human body, crow head. Warrior spirits, masters of forbidden arts. Watchers teaching forbidden knowledge.

- *Mesoamerican – Quetzalcóatl*

Feathered serpent. God of wisdom and creation. Parallel to the "serpent of knowledge."

- *African – Mami Wata / Mermaids*

Half human, half fish. Seductresses linked to wealth and deception. Influence of seductive Watcher spirits.

- *Celtic / Norse – Selkies*

Seal-human shape-shifters. Dual nature and tragedy. Symbol of hybrid identity.

- *Filipino / Asian – Tikbalang*

Human body, horse head. Trickster and deceiver. Demonic hybrid parallel.

Almost every ancient culture describes beings half human and half animal, often tied to forbidden unions, divine punishments, or corrupted wisdom.

These stories echo the account of Genesis 6 and Chănôk concerning the Nefelîm and the Watchers.

Scripture does not lie — we are the blind ones who fail to see the reality and the Nephilim remnant throughout the world.

These wicked beings corrupted all creation of Yahuah by uniting with beasts, reptiles, and birds, creating a series of deformities in creation — entirely hybrid and evil.

A creation that was not part of Yahuah's work, but one formed on earth yet utterly wicked, originated through the women and the Watcher Angels.

They began to devour the creation of Yahuah Êlôhîym until they almost consumed it completely.

And when there were no humans left to devour, they began to devour one another.

Sin, for the first time, reached such a scale that the presence of Yahuah Êlôhîym was provoked.

2.5 Chănôk (Enoch) and the Covenant of Purity

(The birth of the man who walked with Yahuah and was taken without seeing death.)

Then Yahuah sent forth the birth of an extraordinary man into humanity — Chănôk (Enoch), who was set apart by Yahuah Êlôhîym for his purity.

Yahuah issued judgment against the Watcher Angels who sinned and corrupted themselves — those who despised their eternal state in the heavens — using Chănôk as His instrument.

He commanded Chănôk to tell them that because of the multitude of their sins, they would never again speak with Yahuah Êlôhîym — their communication forever cut off — nor lift their eyes to the heavens because of the accursed offspring they had created.

He declared that, just as they had delighted in their evil creation, they would watch their own beloved children be devoured and annihilated, and as fathers they would behold the destruction of their cherished sons without being able to intervene.

Then the Watchers pleaded with Chănôk, the man, to intercede for them before Yahuah Êlôhîym; but Yahuah sent word that no petition would be heard — there would be no redemption, forgiveness, or mercy for their great sin nor for that of their children.

Chănôk (Enoch) 13 : 5
"For from thenceforward they could not speak with him nor lift up their eyes to shâmayim for shame of their sins for which they had been condemned."

Chănôk (Enoch) 14 : 4–7
"I wrote out your petition, and in my vision it appeared thus, that your petition will not be granted unto you throughout all the days of eternity, and that judgement has been finally passed upon you: Yeah your petition will not be granted unto you. And from henceforth you shall not ascend into shâmayim unto all eternity, and in bonds of the earth the decree has gone forth to bind you for all the days of the world. And that previously you shall have seen the destruction of your beloved sons and you shall have no pleasure in them, but they shall fall before you by the sword. And your petition on their behalf shall not be granted, nor yet on your own: even though you weep and pray and speak all the words contained in the writing which I have written".

Chănôk (Enoch) 15: 2
"And go, say to the Watchers of shâmayim, who have sent you to
intercede for them: You should intercede
for men, and not men for you."

The Watcher Angels who once dwelt with Yahuah Êlôhîym could no longer lift their eyes to the heavens because of the great sin they had committed.

Angels had been created to intercede for men — but something unthinkable happened: those same angels now sought a man (Chănôk) to intercede for them.

They wrote their petitions and gave them to Chănôk so that a human might present them to Yahuah Êlôhîym. But the sin was already consummated and the sentence already declared. No plea for mercy or forgiveness — neither for their sins nor for their evil children — would ever be heard.

Before the Watcher Angels were imprisoned in dark dungeons, they would see their children exterminated and would be powerless to stop it. Their beloved sons would be destroyed before their eyes. They had wanted their children to live forever, to share in eternity — this was the desire of the Watcher Angels.

Chănôk (Enoch) 12: 4–6
"Chănôk, you scribe of righteousness, go, declare to the Watchers
of the shâmayim who have left the high shâmayim, the Qâdôsh
eternal place, and have defiled themselves with women, and have
done as the children of earth do, and have taken unto themselves
women: You have wrought great destruction on the earth: And
you shall have no peace nor forgiveness of sin: And inasmuch as
they delight themselves in their children, The murder of their
beloved ones shall they see, and over the destruction of their
children shall they lament, and shall make supplication unto
eternity, but mercy and peace you shall not attain."

Chapter 3
Fallen humanity, corrupted earth, imminent judgment

(When the wickedness of man reached its fullness and the earth was filled with violence)

3.1 State of humanity before the Deluge

This is the state of humanity after the birth of the sons of the women and the Watcher angels, those we know as Nephilim.

Yôbêl (Jubilees) Chapter 5: Verses 2–5:
"And lawlessness increased on the earth and all flesh corrupted its way, alike men and cattle and beasts and birds and everything that walks on the earth, all of them corrupted their ways and their orders, and they began to devour each other, and lawlessness increased on the earth and every imagination of the thoughts of all men was thus evil continually. And Êlôhîym looked upon the earth, and behold it was corrupt, and all flesh had corrupted its orders, and all that were upon the earth had wrought all manner of evil before his eyes. And he said that he would destroy man and all flesh upon the face of the earth which he had created. But Nôach found grace before the eyes of Yahuah."

Let us briefly analyze some points of the text, to see if we truly understand what is happening and what really took place—not what we imagine nor what we have been told, but what the Scriptures actually say.

We have just seen that the Nephilim were exterminating or devouring humans (the creation of Yahuah). The Nephilim were the ones who corrupted themselves and defiled themselves with all men, livestock, beasts, etc. It was not the man created by Yahuah; it was the creation of the women and the Watcher angels. And this imagination or thought continually toward evil is the Nephilim thought (they do not have the gene of the spirit of Yahuah); the Nephilim acted and corrupted all creation.

The reason for the destruction or judgment of extermination does not have to do with the humans whom Yahuah Êlôhîym created; it has to do with the diabolical race created by the women and the Watcher angels.

3.2 Birth of Nôach

(The one born under celestial signs to break the curse of the Watchers and renew the holy lineage)

Chănôk (Enoch) Chapter 106: Verses 1–3:
"And after some days my son Methûshelach took a woman for his son Lemek, and she became pregnant by him and bore a son. And his body was white as snow and red as the blooming of a rose, and the hair of his head and his long locks were white as wool, and his eyes beautiful. And when he opened his eyes, he lighted up the whole house like the sun, and the whole house was very bright. And thereupon he arose in the hands of the midwoman, opened his mouth, and conversed with Yahuah Tsedâqâh."

This is the most incredible birth I have seen in the Scriptures—the birth of Nôach (Noah). The father Lemek even runs out because he thinks he is not his son, because of the astonishing way he was born; but this child had a clear purpose from Yahuah. The child is born and immediately is born speaking with Yahuah. I think even I would run out with something like that.

Chănôk (Enoch) Chapter 106: Verses 15–16, 18:
"Yea, there shall come a great destruction over the whole earth,
and there shall be a deluge and a great destruction for one year.
And this son who has been born unto you shall be left on the
earth, and his three children shall be saved with him: When all
mankind that are on the earth shall die, he and his sons shall be
saved. And now make known to your son Lemek that he who
has been born is in truth his son, and call his name Nôach; for he
shall be left to you, and he and his sons shall be saved from the
destruction, which shall come upon the earth on account of all
the sin and all the unrighteousness, which shall be consummated
on the earth in his days."

This is the prophecy of the birth of Nôach, who would then become
the father of all humanity.

3.3 Announcement of the Deluge

(Yahuah pronounces judgment against the accursed creation).

Yahuah then raised up another creature: Nôach, who was
exceptional from his birth, entirely pure. He was born
speaking and worshiping Yahuah from his very first instant
of life; his face was like that of an angel, radiant and luminous.

Berēshīth (Genesis) — Chapter 6: Verses 13, 17–18:
"And ĔLÔHÎYM said unto Nôach, The end of all flesh is come
before me; for the earth is filled with violence through them; and,
behold, I will destroy them with the earth. And, behold, I, even
I, do bring a flood of waters upon the earth, to destroy all flesh,
wherein is the breath of life, from under heaven; and everything
that is in the earth shall die. But with you I will establish my
covenant; and you shall come into the ark, you, and your sons,
and your wife, and your sons' wives with you."

"For the earth is filled with violence through them." Let us see if we are reading what Berēshīṯh (Genesis) says; violence because of whom? Because of the Nephilim. If you read the context of the chapter you will realize that the narrative is clear: that violence and wickedness is not because of the human being whom Yahuah created; it is because of the Nephilim, the accursed race and aberrant creation that came from the woman and the Watcher angels.

Yahuah is saving the only thing that remains pure from all His creation, because the rest was completely devoured by the Nephilim.

And I repeat it once more so we may understand: the destruction, the wickedness is not because of the human created by Yahuah; it is because of the hybrid being created by the women and the Watcher angels—that is, by the Nephilim.

Yôbêl (Jubilees) Chapter 5: Verses 21–22:
"And he commanded Nôach to make him an ark that he might save himself from the waters of the flood. And Nôach made the ark in all respects as he commanded him, in the twenty seventh jubilee of years, in the fifth week in the fifth year on the beginning of the first month."

Yahuah commanded Nôach to build the ark because He was going to destroy that accursed creation—never His human creation, but the accursed creation, the sons of the women and of the Watcher Angels.

3.4 The Boats of the Nefelîn

(Before the flood, the sons of the Watchers tried to escape the divine decree with their own vessels)

The flood was no secret: the Watcher angels knew of the decreed judgment, and likewise they sent their sons to build boats.

The boats or ships of the Nephilim—sons of the Watcher angels—were made with metal, but the ark that Yahuah commanded Nôach to build was entirely of wood.

Nôach built one ark, but the Nephilim built hundreds of ships to try to escape the judgment that had been decreed against that accursed, completely corrupt creation which had destroyed all the creation of Yahuah.

In the book of the Nephilim demon Enki (The Lost Book of Enki), an occult (NON-BIBLICAL) book, one can find the account or episode where the Anaqiy or Anunnaki build many boats trying to have their Nephilim sons escape—and all were drowned, with the exception of one.

"The purpose of the boat, a secret of the Anunnaki, must remain with you!" Page 170. "Let us descend in Whirlwinds from the celestial boats upon the summit of Arrata," page 175. "In their Whirlwinds they flew over the other summit of Arrata, they saw the boat of Ziusudra, and beside the altar that he had built they disembarked."

Before that destruction, Yahuah decided to take Chănôk to the garden of Eden or to paradise alive, with a prophetic purpose for the end of days.

All those generations before the flood died: the generation of Yârad, of Chănôk, Methûshâêl, and Lemek; only the generation of Nôach remained—his wife, his sons, and his sons' wives: eight persons in total.

All the rest of humanity was in complete corruption by the Nephilim, descendants of the women and of the Watcher Angels;

entirely wicked and without the "chip" of spiritual connection to draw near to Yahuah, bearing only the carnal, diabolical, and destructive chip.

3.5 Deluge

(The purification of the earth and the rescue of the pure lineage of Nôach).

The flood was sent and all that accursed race was exterminated—or, rather, almost all of that race.

Yôbêl (Jubilees) Chapter 7: Verses 21–24:
"For owing to these three things came the flood upon the earth, namely, owing to the fornication wherein the Watchers against the law of their ordinances went a whoring after the daughters of men, and took themselves women of all which they chose: and they made the beginning of uncleanness. And they begat sons the Nâphîdîm, and they were all unlike, and they devoured one another: and the Nephiyl slew the Nâphîl, and the Nâphîl slew the Elyô, and the Elyô mankind, and one man another. And every one sold himself to work iniquity and to shed much blood, and the earth was filled with iniquity. And after this they sinned against the beasts and birds, and all that moves and walks on the earth: And much blood was shed on the earth, and every imagination and desire of men imagined vanity and evil continually."

Summary of the three causes:

1. Union of the Watchers with the women.

2. They begot impure children—different in forms and sizes. Origin of impurity.

3. The sin of those creatures against all creation.

Nôach and his family, eight members in total, were the only

survivors of the pure human race and creation of Yahuah, together with all the species of animals that were preserved in the ark with Nôach. But...

3.4 A family of the Nephilim that survived the flood

(The origin of the Nephilim kingdoms after the flood.)

What they have never told you nor expressed is that, of the hundreds of ships of the Nephilim, all were drowned and destroyed with the exception of one family of the Nephilim that survived the flood; whose boat ran aground in the mountains of Arrata, in Turkey.

The son of the extraterrestrial god—or rather, of the demon or Watcher angel who corrupted himself—known as Enki, along with his son and family, survived.

However, the ark of Nôach ran aground in another part of the mountains, bordering Armenia, or rather, on the other side of the mountains of Ararat, on the highest peak in the world, known as Mount Lubar, within the Himalayan ranges—what we today know as Mount Everest.

Yôbêl (Jubilees) — Chapter 5: Verse 28:
"And the ark went and rested on the top of Lûbâr, one of the mountains of Ărârat."

Jubilees tells you the same as Berēšhīth: in the mountains of Ararat, and it gives you the specific place, which is the summit of Lubar. Let us see what Lubar is or where it is found.

Berēšhīth (Genesis) — Chapter 8: Verse 4:
"And the ark rested in the seventh month, on the seventeenth day of the month, upon the mountains of Ărârat".

Berēshīṯh tells you that the ark of Nôach ran aground upon the mountains (mountains... several, not one) of Ararat—understand that it is a mountainous region, and on one of the mountains of Ararat it ran aground—and it specifies the highest of all humanity.

Berēshīṯh (Genesis) — Chapter 7: Verse 19:
"And the waters prevailed exceedingly upon the earth; and all the high hills, that were under the whole heaven, were covered."

The confusion lies in the plural of the words, and this is the tool of lies that the enemy has used to confuse and to hide the place where the ark of the Nephilim (Mount Ararat) ran aground—and not the ark of Nôach.

"Mount Ararat is located in the far east of Turkey, very close to the borders with Armenia and Iran."

Let us look at historical evidence of the existence of Lubar. "Mummery's party had crossed this Mazeno pass, at 5,400 meters, and had descended to Lubar, at the head of the Bunar valley. Page 11. In the end the rest of us joined Collie and Raghobir and we all descended by the Lubar glacier, about 2,100 meters below the pass, to the shepherds' settlement in the Alp of Lubar, so to speak. Page 14. The day I spent skirting the great ridge that separated me from the Alp of Lubar was anything but monotonous. Page 15."

And remember that it is the memory of the Himalaya; therefore we understand that Lubar is part of the Himalaya and that it borders Turkey and Armenia (Armenia is part of the great Alpine-Himalayan mountain range). There are many high mountains on the borders of China, India, and Nepal (where the ark of Nôach ran aground), precisely on Everest, which is the highest mountain in the world, although there are more than a hundred high mountains—that is the highest in the world.

Ărâraṭ: or rather Armenia. A mountainous region of eastern

Armenia, between the river Araxes and the lakes Van and Oroomiah, the place where the ark of Noah came to rest.

Armenia is situated in southern Transcaucasia and covers the northeast part of the Armenian highlands (situated in the Alpine-Himalayan range). Armenia is landlocked and borders Georgia to the north, Azerbaijan to the east, Turkey to the west, and Iran to the south. From the late Middle Ages (1492), the Ararat of the ark has been identified with the present-day Mount Ararat in Turkey.

As you can see, it is part of the campaign of lies and deceit of the descendants of the Nephilim. Only from 1492 onward do they begin the campaign of the great deception, preaching and teaching the ark of the Nephilim as if it were that of Nôach, when in reality it is the ark of the demons that they have taught.

The Himalaya (from Sanskrit हिमालय, himālaya [pronounced jimaalaia], where hima, "snow," and ālaya, "abode," "place") is a mountain range located on the Asian continent, and it extends through several countries: Bhutan, Nepal, China, Burma, India, and Pakistan.

It is the highest mountain range on Earth, with 8,850 m a.s.l. in height, according to the most recent measurement, published in December 2020. There are more than one hundred summits exceeding 7,000 meters and fourteen summits of more than 8,000 meters in height.

But only one fulfills the biblical description of the highest summit in the world: "Mount Everest or Éverest is the highest mountain on the surface of planet Earth, with an altitude of 8,848.86 meters (29,032 feet) above sea level."

Chapter 4
Bodiless shadows that wander the earth since the days of the Deluge

(The sons of chaos who torment humanity)

4.1 Demons or evil angels

(The wandering spirits born of the forbidden union).

When all the sons of the women with the Watcher Angels, namely, the Nephilim were exterminated, because they were not part of creation, they had no place to go or to rest.

Men have their dwelling on the earth, and when they die, they go to their place of rest; angels do not die.

But all these dead hybrids became what we know today as evil spirits or demons.

The union of the women with the Watcher Angels brought forth a deformed and entirely evil race, which was almost annihilated in its entirety.

The spirits of these dead ones, having no place anywhere in creation, were left to wander over the earth: these are the evil spirits or demons.

They were created on the earth; therefore, their dwelling is on the earth.

They were created by humans (women and Watcher Angels), and for that reason they torment the human race. They do not eat or drink, but they are always hungry and thirsty.

Chănôk (Enoch) - Chapter 15: Verse 8–12:
"And now, the nephîyl, who are produced from the spirits and

flesh, shall be called evil spirits upon the earth, and on the earth shall be their dwelling. Evil spirits have proceeded from their bodies; because they are born from men and from the qâdôsh Watchers is their beginning and primal origin; they shall be evil spirits on earth, and evil spirits shall they be called. As for the spirits of shâmayim, in shâmayim shall be their dwelling, but as for the spirits of the earth which were born upon the earth, on the earth shall be their dwelling.And the spirits of the nephîyl afflict, oppress, destroy, attack, do battle, and work destruction on the earth, and cause trouble: They take no food, but nevertheless hunger and thirst, and cause offences. And these spirits shall rise up against the children of men and against the women, because they have proceeded from them."

These are the forerunners of all evil and all disease in the human race.

Before this aberration or accursed creation—before the death of these hybrid and evil beings—there were no demons nor diseases.

All were brought by the demons, the product or result of the union of the women with the Watcher Angels, who, wishing to create their own offspring, begot the worst aberration that wiped out the human race and will, once again, bring an end to this creation.

4.2 What is the perdition of humanity?

(The cause behind the fall of man.)

Humanity remains hypnotized and dazzled by the teachings and supposed sciences of the Watchers. And in many cases, brothers in Yahuah as well, not understanding that the cause of all destruction was those teachings and in the end, those same teachings will lead to destruction by fire.

Chănôk (Enoch) - Chapter 10: Verse 7–8, 15:
*"And heal the earth which the angels have corrupted, and
proclaim the healing of the earth, that they may heal the plague,
and that all the children of men may not perish through all the
secret things that the Watchers have disclosed and have taught
their sons. And the whole earth has been corrupted through the
works that were taught by Ăzâzêl: To him ascribe all sin. And
destroy all the spirits of the reprobate and the children of the
Watchers, because they have wronged mankind."*

Chănôk (Enoch) - Chapter 16: Verse 3:
*They were in the shamayim, but not all the mysteries had yet
been revealed to them, and they knew some that were of no
value; and in the hardness of their hearts they have made them
known to the women, and by these mysteries women and men
cause much evil upon the earth.*

Chănôk (Enoch) - Chapter 19: Verse 1:
*"And Ûrîyêl said to me: Here shall stand the angels who have
connected themselves with women, and their spirits assuming
many different forms are defiling mankind and shall lead them
astray into sacrificing to demons as gods, here they shall stand,
till the day of the great judgement in which they shall be judged
till they are made an end of."*

Chănôk (Enoch) - Chapter 65: Verse 11:
*"And these, they have no place of repentance forever, because
they have shown them what was hidden, and they are the
damned: But as for you, my son, Yahuah of Rûach knows that*

you are pure, and guiltless of this reproach concerning the
secrets."

I do not think the Scriptures could be clearer—or is it that we do not want to see or understand? All these supposed sciences and teachings that were not destined for humans to learn and that were taught by the Watchers and their women, all lead to the same path: "destruction."

4.3 Maśṭêmâh through the Generations

(The angel of judgment and the testing of man).

Maśṭêmâh is a powerful angel mentioned in the Scriptures, about whom little has been revealed, and around whom there are many confusions and distorted teachings.

For a long time it has been said that it was not he who deceived Chawwâh (Eve) in the garden, but another being called Gadreel or Gadriel.

However, when observing the ancient writings more closely, the possibility arises that both names refer to the same rebellious spirit—the one who rose against the truth from the beginning and sowed corruption in the creation of Yahuah.

Who is this figure and why is it important to know him? In traditional Bibles, this figure has been completely hidden, but in reality he has a role that we all should know.

His first mention as such is found in the book of Hosea, and obviously to see it you have to look at the original Hebrew or read it in Dâbâr Yahuah – Yahuah Scriptures.

Hôshêa (Hosea) - Chapter 9: Verse 7–8:
"The days of visitation are come, the days of recompense
are come; Yâshârêl shall know it: the prophet is a fool, the
rûach man is mad, for the multitude of your iniquity, and the

prince Maśṭêmâh. The watchman of Ephrayim was with my ĔLÔHÎYM: but the prophet is a snare of a fowler in all his ways, and Maśṭêmâh in the house of his ĔLÔHÎYM."

If you read the full context of this chapter you will understand that Yahuah is decreeing His judgment because of the multitude of wickedness and because of the prince Maśṭêmâh, for they have him in the house of Êlôhîym, usurping the place of Êlôhîym.

Maśṭêmâh: translates as enmity or hatred.

However, this real figure appears throughout the Scriptures.

In the Book of Jubilees, Maśṭêmâh is mentioned as the leader of the evil spirits who survived the Deluge, the one who asked Yahuah for permission to test men and lead them away from the path of righteousness.

On the other hand, in the Book of Chănôk (Enoch), Gadreel is named as the one who seduced Chawwâh and taught men the art of war and destruction.

Both are described as instigators of evil, enemies of the truth, and bearers of corrupted knowledge.

Therefore, it is not far-fetched to think that Maśṭêmâh and Gadreel are the same spirit manifested under different names, fulfilling the same mission: to deceive, destroy, and oppose the eternal purpose of Yahuah from the beginning to the end.

Now let us look at the references so that we may come out of deception and blindness, and see if we can understand who Maśṭêmâh is and what his true role in humanity is.

4.4 Maśṭêmâh and his henchmen

(The leader of the fallen spirits who still roam the earth).

Maśțêmâh is the angel in charge of all evil spirits or demons—the 10% that he asked permission from Yahuah—and he still roams the earth.

He has not been judged; he continues fulfilling his functions and has constant access to the heaven, to the presence of Yahuah Êlôhîym.

Yôbêl (Jubilees) - Chapter 10: Verse 8-9:
"And the chief of the spirits, Mastêmâ, came and said: Yahuah, Bârâ, let some of them remain before me, and let them harken to my voice, and do all that I shall say unto them; for if some of them are not left to me, I shall not be able to execute the power of my will on the sons of men; for these are for corruption and leading astray before my judgment, for great is the wickedness of the sons of men. And he said: Let the tenth part of them remain before him, and let nine parts descend into the place of condemnation."

Yahuah, as punishment, imprisoned all the Watcher Angels who corrupted themselves with the women, shutting them up in dark prisons until the day of the final judgment.

And when He was about to imprison all the demons together with their fathers, Maśțêmâh—who is not a fallen angel, but an angel with a specific purpose—interceded before Yahuah and asked Him to assign him 10% of those demons in order to fulfill the task that had been entrusted to him.

Yôbêl (Jubilees) - Chapter 11: Verse 4–5:
"And they made for themselves molten images, and they worshipped each the idol, the molten image which they had made for themselves, and they began to make graven images and unclean simulacra, and malignant spirits assisted and seduced them into committing transgression and uncleanness. And the

prince Mastêmâ exerted himself to do all this, and he sent forth other spirits, those which were put under his hand, to do all manner of wrong and sin, and all manner of transgression, to corrupt and destroy, and to shed blood upon the earth."

Yahuah granted his request, and Maśṭêmâh became the leader of the 10% of the demons who roam the earth, always seeking whom to devour, tormenting and attacking the sons of men and the women from whom they proceed.

Only 10% were left free; the remaining 90% are in dark prisons.

4.5 Maśṭêmâh and the ravens rebuked by Abraham

(The prince of darkness confronted by the faith of the righteous).

Yôbêl (Jubilees) - Chapter 11: Verse 18–21:
"And the time of sowing came, and they all went out together to protect their seed from the ravens. Abraham went out with those who went, and the child was a lad of fourteen years. A cloud of ravens came to devour the seed, and Abraham ran to meet them before they alighted upon the ground, and he cried out to them before they alighted upon the ground to devour the seed, and he said to them: "Do not come down; return to the place from which you came." And they proceeded to return. And he made the clouds of ravens return that day seventy times, and of all the ravens in all the land where Abraham was, not one alighted there. And all who were with him in all the land saw him cry out, and all the ravens turned back; and his name became great in all the land of Kaśđıy."

Thisis one of the first feats of Abraham in his youth. Abraham then rebukes the ravens sent by the prince Maśṭêmâh throughout the whole day, and in the end, all depart after being rebuked.

Chapter 5
Faith against accusation
(The heavenly dialogue that unleashed the test of sacrifice)

5.1 Maṣṭêmâh asks to test Abraham

(The challenge to sacrifice Yitschâq).

A braham had already involved himself in the affairs of the prince Maṣṭêmâh, leader of all the demons.

> *Berēshīṯh (Genesis) — Chapter 22: Verses 1, 2, 9–12:*
> "And it came to pass after these things, that ĔLÔHÎYM did tempt Abrâhâm, and said unto him, Abrâhâm: and he said, Behold, here I am. And he said, Take now your son, your only son Yitschâq, whom you love, and get you into the land of Môrîyâh; and offer him there for a burnt offering upon one of the mountains which I will tell you of. And they came to the place which ĔLÔHÎYM had told him of; and Abrâhâm built an altar there, and laid the wood in order, and bound Yitschâq his son, and laid him on the altar upon the wood. And he said, Lay not your hand upon the lad, neither do you anything unto him: for now I know that you fear ĔLÔHÎYM, seeing you have not withheld your son, your only son from me."

We all know the account of Abraham—or rather, we think we know it well—but only when we compare the account in the Book of Jubilees we can grasp the magnitude of what truly happened.

> *Yôbêl (Jubilees) — Chapter 17: Verse 16:*
> "And the prince Mastêmâ came and said before Êlôhîym, behold, Abrâhâm loves Yitschâq his son, and he delights in him above all things else; bid him to offer him as a burnt offering on the altar,

and you will see if he will do this command, and you will know if
he is faithful in everything wherein you do try him."

Yôbêl (Jubilees) — Chapter 18: Verses 9–11
"And I stood before him, and before the prince Mastêmâ, and
Yahuah said, do not bid him to lay his hand on the lad, nor to
do anything to him, for I have shown that he fears Yahuah. And
I called to him from shâmayim, and said unto him: Abrâhâm,
Abrâhâm; and he was terrified and said: Behold, here I am. And I
said unto him: Do not lay your hand upon the lad, neither you do
nothing to him; for now I have shown that you fear Yahuah, and
have not withheld your son, your first born son, from me."

Do we understand what truly happens behind the scenes? Maśtêmâh is the one who asks to test Abraham, and Yahuah grants the request; and Abraham passes the test of the prince Maśtêmâh and, by his act of faith, put Maśtêmâh to ridicule and shame.

Let us pay close attention so our eyes may be opened to the truth and to the understanding that Yahuah sets before us.

5.2 Abraham blesses Yaqoob

(Yahuah's promise of protection against the spirits of Maśtêmâh)

When Abraham is pronouncing his blessing over Yaăqôb, he says this:

Yôbêl (Jubilees) — Chapter 19: Verse 28:
"And the spirits of Mastêmâ shall not rule over you or over
your seed to turn you from Yahuah, who is your Êlôhîym from
henceforth forever."

Abraham knows and recognizes who the commander of all the

demons is. We are the ones who have lost that knowledge—or it has been kept hidden from us so that we would not know. What a beautiful and wise blessing. But this is not all; we continue with the exploits involving Maśṭêmâh.

5.3 Maśṭêmâh tries to kill Môsheh (Moses)

(The adversary in the shadow of the exodus).

I always wondered and never clearly understood what this passage meant; truth be told, I never grasped this event in the Scriptures until I read it in the Book of Jubilees.

Šhemōṯh (Exodus) — Chapter 4: Verses 24–26
"And it came to pass by the way in the inn, that YAHUAH met him, and sought to kill him. Then Tsippôrâh took a sharp stone, and cut off the foreskin of her son, and cast it at his feet, and said, surely a bloody husband are you to me. So he let him go: then she said a bloody husband you are, because of the circumcision."

How is it that Yahuah met him and sought to kill him? However, it was Yahuah himself who sent him to deliver His people. Then how is it that He would try to kill His emissary Môsheh? Exodus says that Yahuah met Môsheh and sought to kill him. Yet if Yahuah had wanted him dead, He would not have sent him, nor would He have rescued Môsheh from childhood. Something was always missing in this story; something was not right. Let us now read it in Jubilees.

Yôbêl (Jubilees) — Chapter 48: Verses 2–4: "And you yourself know what he spoke unto you on Mount Sıynay, and what prince Mastêmâ desired to do with you when you were returning into Mitsrayim on the way when you did meet him at the lodging place. Did he not with all his power seek to slay you and deliver the Mitsŕıy out of your hand when he saw that you were sent to execute judgment and vengeance on the Mitsŕiy? And I delivered you out of his hand, and you did perform the signs and wonders which you were sent to perform in Mitsrayim against Parôh, and against all his house, and against his servants and his people."

Now everything makes sense; now I can truly understand what happened. Maśṭêmâh was commanding the Egyptians, and when he saw that Yahuah had sent Môsheh to deliver His people, he tried to kill Môsheh on the way in order to free Mitsrayim (Egypt).

5.4 Maśṭêmâh with the Egyptians

(The spirit of destruction that opposed Yâshârêl).

Understand that the people of Yâshârêl were slaves in Egypt, and that the prince Maśṭêmâh stood as leader of the Egyptians, working oppression through the Egyptians against Yâshârêl.

Yôbêl (Jubilees) — Chapter 48: Verses 9–13:
"And the prince Mastêmâ stood up against you, and sought to cast you into the hands of Parôh, and he helped the Mitsŕiy sorcerers, and they stood up and wrought before you. The evils indeed we permitted them to work, but the remedies we did not allow to be wrought by their hands. And Yahuah smote them with malignant ulcers, and they were not able to stand, for we destroyed them so that they could not perform a single sign. And notwithstanding all these signs and wonders the prince Mastêmâ was not put to shame because he took courage and cried to the Mitsŕiy to pursue after you with all the powers of the Mitsŕiy, with their chariots, and with their horses, and with all the hosts of the peoples of Mitsrayim. And I stood between the Mitsŕiy and Yâshârêl, and we delivered Yâshârêl out of his hand, and out of the hand of his people, and Yahuah brought them through the

midst of the sea as if it were dry land."

We have always read that Yahuah hardened Pharaoh's heart to display His power; however, Jubilees shows us the full panorama, how the prince Maśṭêmâh is behind the Egyptians, and Yahuah uses their pride to harden the heart of Pharaoh and the Egyptians in order to display His marvelous power.

5.5 Maśṭêmâh bound and the people delivered

(Judgment upon the adversary during the redemption of Yâshârêl).

The influence of Maśṭêmâh was so great over the people who serve Maśṭêmâh (Egypt) that it was necessary to bind Maśṭêmâh to free the people of Yâshârêl.

Yôbêl (Jubilees) — Chapter 48: Verses 15–18:
"And on the fourteenth day and on the fifteenth and on the sixteenth and on the seventeenth and on the eighteenth the prince Mastêmâ was bound and imprisoned behind the children of Yâshârêl that he might not accuse them. And on the nineteenth we let them loose that they might help the Mitsrıy and pursue the children of Yâshârêl. And he hardened their hearts and made them stubborn, and the device was devised by Yahuah our Êlôhîym that he might smite the Mitsrıy and cast them into the sea. And on the fourteenth we bound him that he might not accuse the children of Yâshârêl on the day when they asked the Mitsrıy for vessels and garments, vessels of silver, and vessels of gold, and vessels of bronze, in order to despoil the Mitsrıy in return for the bondage in which they had forced them to serve."

5.6 Maśṭêmâh kills all the firstborn of Egypt

(The execution of final judgment upon the enemies of Yahuah).

But the greatest test had not yet passed. We have read how Yahuah struck all the firstborn of Egypt. And Exodus tells us that Yahuah would pass through striking them, but that He would not allow the destroyer to enter the houses of Yâshârêl. Thus we understand and know, and are 100% clear that Yahuah is not the destroyer—this destroyer has his name.

Šhemōṯh (Exodus) — Chapter 12: Verses 23, 29:
"And you shall take a bunch of hyssop, and dip it in the blood that is in the bason, and strike the lintel and the two side posts with the blood that is in the bason; and none of you shall go out at the door of his house until the morning. For YAHUAH will pass through to smite the Mitsrayim; and when he sees the blood upon the lintel, and on the two side posts, YAHUAH will pass over the door, and will not suffer the destroyer to come in unto your houses to smite you."

Now we can clearly see who executed the order to kill all the firstborn in Egypt.

Yôbêl (Jubilees) — Chapter 49: Verse 2:
"For on this night, the beginning of the festival and the beginning of the joy, you were eating the Pesach in Mitsrayim, when all the powers of Mastêmâ had been let loose to slay all the first born in the land of Mitsrayim, from the first born of Parôh to the first born of the captive maidservant in the mill, and to the cattle."

We can say with clarity and certainty that the executioners behind the death of the firstborn were Maṣṭêmâh and his henchmen.

5.7 "Satan": the nonexistent... and imposed enemy

(The great invention that hid the identity of the true adversary.)

W e still lack clarity regarding the role or identity of the figure Maśṭêmâh. Let us analyze one of the best-told lies in humanity.

Throughout history we have been taught many things, and one of them is that there exists a supposed enemy or arch-enemy of Yahuah and of the people of Yahuah, whom we must fear, rebuke, and so forth. But let us look at reality now.

The Hebrew term is śâṭân (שָׂטָן): it means "adversary," "opponent," or "accuser," and that is how it is used in the Scriptures—except in places where its meaning was distorted to confuse humanity, presenting it as an "arch-enemy" of Yahuah.

But Yahuah has no such enemy, because nothing and no one can oppose Him.

You can read each of these verses, and if you read the Hebrew you will notice that the term used is the same, but here it was translated as it truly is—adversary—and not as an unreal proper name. (Numbers 22:22; 1 Samuel 29:4; 1 Kings 5:4; 1 Kings 11:14, 23 & 25).

However, in each of these other verses it has been translated as a proper name—erroneously or knowingly—trying to create a figure that in reality does not exist. (1 Chronicles 21:1; Job 1:6, 7, 8, 9, 10; Job 2:1, 2, 3, 4, 6, 7; Psalms 19:6; Zechariah 3:1 & 2).

Let us look at some of the verses in the book of Job, where most often it has been rendered as a proper name instead of the real term "adversary." Since we are using the Dâbâr Yahuah – Yahuah Scriptures version, it has the correct term, so let us pay attention.

Îyôb (Job) — Chapter 1: Verses 6–7: "Now there was a day when the sons of ĔLÔHÎYM came to present themselves before YAHUAH, and the Adversary came also among them. And YAHUAH said unto the Adversary, Whence come you? Then the Adversary answered YAHUAH, and said, from going to and fro in the earth, and from walking up and down in it."

We will read only the first two verses, since we know the story well, though you may read the entire chapter for better understanding.

Among the sons of Êlôhîym—understand, the angels—there comes a specific figure: the adversary. If you see this story and compare it with that of Abraham, you will better understand and realize we are speaking about the same figure—the adversary—who comes into the presence of Yahuah.

Remember: he is not a Watcher angel, nor did he corrupt himself with the women. All the Watcher angels who corrupted themselves are confined in eternal prisons, and from the moment of their sin they could no longer speak with Yahuah, nor present themselves before Yahuah, nor ascend to the shamayim. This is the same one we have already seen in the lives of Abraham, Môsheh, and now in Îyôb (Job), testing the faithful servant of Yahuah.

And the most important part you must always keep in mind is that this adversary—better known as Maśṭêmâh, whom they have wrongly called "satan"—his true name is Maśṭêmâh. He has been present since ancient times, and part of his task has been to test the followers of Yahuah to see whether they will fall into his snares or remain faithful to Yahuah.

This same adversary can be seen throughout the history of humanity and we shall see him later in the New Testament as well, for his work, role, or office will be fulfilled at the end of days. In the meantime, he is an angel inhabiting the earth who has access to the throne of Yahuah, and who can be in only one place at a time; thus, in whatever nation he is found, he is there in bodily presence.

To clarify for better understanding: the one they have called "satan" throughout the centuries—that is not his name, since the term only means adversary. However, the true Adversary is named Maśṭêmâh.

Chapter 6
The Power of Demons

*(How Unclean Spirits Dominate
Through Fear and Ignorance)*

6.1 The Nature and Limits of Demonic Power

These demons do not possess the kind of power people attribute to them; they are not corporeal beings, and their only ability is to inhabit or possess other bodies, since they themselves lack one.

The power of demons lies in subtle influence and deceptive information, which they use to lead people into sin — that is, to induce the followers of Yahuah into disobedience.

Demons cannot, nor are they permitted to, touch or possess a servant of Yahuah. However, they do have the ability to possess, influence, guide, and direct their human descendants — that is, the nephilim descendants who still dwell among us and whose ways are continually toward evil. They inhabit and use them freely because they are part of their lineage.

We must remember that demons are ancestral spirits; therefore, they know human behavior better than humans themselves — through centuries of observation.

That is why the Scriptures speak of familiar spirits, those that move from generation to generation. These same spirits can imitate a person's voice and create realistic scenarios that deceive the senses. And let us not forget — in most cases, demons know the content of Scripture better than we do.

But the one who serves Yahuah has been given power and authority over every evil or familiar spirit. We have the power; they do not.

6.2 The Mermaids

(The Punishment of the Women Who United Themselves With the Watcher Angels)

The women of the Watcher angels who united themselves with them were cursed by Yahuah and transformed into mermaids.

It might sound like a fairy tale or science fiction, but that is precisely what they want people to believe — to hide the truth. We rarely, if ever, speak of those women who were defiled by the Watcher angels. In fact, I have never heard anyone discuss them, yet the Book of Chănôk (Enoch) gives us an astonishing detail: these women also received their punishment for their transgression with the angels and for participating in the creation of that diabolical, aberrant race.

Chănôk (Enoch) 19:2
"And the women also of the angels who went
astray shall become sirens."

If the sirens (mermaids) are the women who joined with the Watcher angels and corrupted their nature, what then would be the offspring of a mermaid? A hybrid nephilim.

That is why, in myths and legends, mermaids are always portrayed as female — they bear within themselves the mark of punishment and curse for their sin.

6.3 The Rebirth of Evil: Babel and the Patriarchs

6.3.1 Migration to Babylon

(The Descendants of the Nephilim After the Flood)

The surviving nephilim descended from Mount Ararat into the lands of Shinar (Senaar or Sinar) and settled there. They began to multiply; this very region later became known as Babel or Babylon. Shinar, Sinar, or Senaar is the ancient name of Babylon.

Berēshiṯh (Genesis) 11:1–9:

"And the whole earth was of one language, and of one speech. And it came to pass, as they journeyed from the east, that they found a plain in the land of Shin'âr; and they dwelt there. And they said one to another, Go, let us make brick, and burn them thoroughly. And they had brick for stone, and slime had they for morter. And they said, Go to, let us build us a city and a tower, whose top may reach unto heaven; and let us make us a name, lest we be scattered abroad upon the face of the whole earth. And YAHUAH came down to see the city and the tower, which the children of men built. And YAHUAH said, Behold, the people is one, and they have all one language; and this they begin to do: and now nothing will be restrained from them, which they have imagined to do. Go to, let us go down, and there confound their language, that they may not understand one another's speech. So YAHUAH scattered them abroad from thence upon the face of all the earth: and they left off to build the city. Therefore is the name of it called Bâbel; because YAHUAH did there confound the language of all the earth: and from thence did YAHUAH scatter them abroad upon the face of all the earth."

Bâbel (לְבָב) means confusion; that is, Babylon, the empire of confusion.

Let us understand what we are reading: in Chapter 10, Nôach (Noah) divided the earth among his sons and their descendants. And let us not forget — this is a record that Môsheh (Moses) wrote of the events that Yahuah revealed to him.

What occurs in Genesis 11 is a recounting of the positioning and rebellion of the nephilim descendants, an attempt to reconnect with the heavens — as their fallen ancestors once did.

6.3.2 Babylon

(The Hybrid Civilization That Defied Heaven)

Shinar, Sinar, or Senaar is the ancient name of Babylon.

Yôbêl (Jubilees) 10:18–25 tells us: "… Peleg took to himself a woman, whose name was Lômnâ the daughter of Shinâr, and she bare him a son in the fourth year of this week, and he called his name Rêû; for he said: Behold the children of men have become evil through the wicked purpose of building for themselves a city and a tower in the land of Shinâr. For this reason the whole land of Shinâr is called Bâbel, because Yahuah did there confound all the language of the children of men, and from thence they were dispersed into their cities, each according to his language and his nation."

These sons of men mentioned in Berēshīth (Genesis) and Jubilees are the same ones who landed upon Mount Ararat (the nephilim) and descended afterward to the land of Shinar. These "sons of men" belong to the second group of humanity, not the first — as we will see in Chapter 7.

Yôbêl (Jubilees) 10:19 "They migrated from the land of Ararat eastward to Sennaar, and at that time built the city and the tower, saying, 'Let us ascend to heaven by it."

Would any human created by Yahuah conceive such madness as to force his way into heaven? Is it not clear that these acts were devised by the nephilim?

Yôbêl (Jubilees) 10:20–26: "And they began to build, and in the fourth week they made brick with fire, and the bricks served them for stone, and the clay with which they cemented them together was asphalt which comes out of the sea, and out of the fountains of water in the land of Shinâr. And they built it: forty and three years were they building it... And Yahuah our Êlôhîym said unto us: Behold, they are one people, and this they begin to do, and now nothing will be withheld from them. Go to, let us go down and confound their language that they may not understand one another's speech, and they may be dispersed into cities and nations, and one purpose will no longer abide with them till the Day of Judgment. And Yahuah descended, and we descended with him to see the city and the tower which the children of men had built. And he confounded their language, and they no longer understood one another's speech, and they ceased then to build the city and the tower. For this reason the whole land of Shinâr is called Bâbel, because Yahuah did there confound all the language of the children of men, and from thence they were dispersed into their cities, each according to his language and his nation. And Yahuah sent a mighty wind against the tower and overthrew it upon the earth, and behold it was between Ashshûr and Bâbel in the land of Shinâr, and they called its name "Overthrow".

6.3.3 The Tower of Babel

(The Attempt to Reach the Divine Throne by Force)

We have never been told the truth.

For centuries we have lived blind and deceived, believing lies — or simply ignorant of reality — thinking that all catastrophes and destructions throughout history were caused by the humans created by Yahuah Êlôhîym. The truth, however, is very different.

The inhabitants who settled in the city of Shinar, also called Babel or Babylon, were the survivors of the Flood — the nephilim (the offspring of the women and the Watcher angels who sinned).

And yes, they were human in appearance — or rather, they had human blood — but they were not 100% part of Yahuah's creation.

They did not possess the spirit that connects with goodness or with Yahuah. The only "chip" they had was the seed of evil.

Thus these descendants of angels and women who lived in Babel multiplied, yet it was decreed that they could never ascend to heaven or call upon Yahuah, because they were an aberration in creation — beings hybrid in nature, half human and half angelic.

Therefore, their purpose was to reach heaven by force, since access was denied to them.

At that time, humanity spoke a single language — Eber (Hebrew). All were in agreement to build a tower that would reach the heavens.

Yahuah saw their purpose and understood that nothing would restrain them. The nephilim and their descendants desired access to heaven, and nothing would stop them from pursuing it.

That was the true purpose of constructing the Tower of Babel.

Then Yahuah descended, destroyed the tower, confused their tongues, and thus the languages of the world were born.

He scattered them across the face of the earth so they would never again unite in a common purpose — for their only goal was destruction and usurpation of the heavens.

Babel and its tower were not destroyed, nor were their languages confounded, because of the pure humans created by Yahuah. No.

It was because of the diabolical creation that resulted from the union of the women and the Watcher angels.

It was never the fault of Yahuah's original creation — but the consequence of rebellion between men (women) and fallen angels.

Babel means "confusion", and true to its name, it will continue to confuse humanity until the end of time, for its origin and purpose are entirely nephilim and opposed to everything good and everything that comes from Yahuah.

Chapter 7
The Two Seeds

(The Pure Line of Yahuah and the Corrupted Lineage of the Nephilim)

The Two Existing Groups in Humanity

(Two lineages, two destinies: one guided by the ruaḥ of Yahuah, and the other by the corruption of the adversary.)

7.1 Two Groups After the Corruption of the Watchers

From the moment the Watcher angels corrupted themselves by uniting with women and creating that aberrant race, and after the destruction of the Flood, humanity on earth was divided into two groups.

Group 1: Humans created by Yahuah Êlôhîym, who carry within them the ruaḥ (spirit) of Yahuah to reproduce and multiply on the earth. They are called "sons of men," but they carry the ruaḥ of Yahuah.

Group 2: Hybrid humans who possess human blood from the women and angelic blood from the Watcher angels. These do not possess the ruaḥ of Yahuah Êlôhîym and are unable to seek anything good, much less Yahuah Himself. They are also called "sons of men," but they do not carry the ruaḥ of Yahuah—for they were born of women and angels, not through divine creation.

7.2 Nephilim Dispersion After Babel

Let us expand on this concept for better understanding. The inhabitants of Babel were nephilim. They sought to reach the heavens by building the tower, but Yahuah destroyed the tower and confused their languages so they could no longer unite in their diabolical purpose.

All these nephilim, who carried both human (female) and angelic (Watcher) blood, were scattered across the known civilizations of that time.

Here begins the great puzzle. At first, the men (humans with nephilim blood) did not pose much danger, because though they bore the spirit of the nephilim, they could not transmit what they did not have — namely, the "divine gene" or "chip" of Yahuah to their descendants.

However, the greatest danger to Yahuah's creation once again came through women. When nephilim women united with men who carried the ruaḥ of Yahuah, the offspring of such unions were born with two spiritual genes or chips: one nephilim (from the mother) and one divine (from the man of Yahuah).

This new being, though still hybrid and containing nephilim blood, for the first time had the opportunity to partake in the divine seed of Yahuah Êlôhîym, because it had been transmitted through the man.

7.3 Prohibitions and Commands Regarding Marriages

This is why Yahuah always forbade His people from marrying women of pagan nations — those with nephilim blood. Likewise, this explains why, during every conquest, Yahuah commanded His people to destroy all inhabitants — from the youngest to the oldest — because they carried the nephilim gene and had to be eradicated.

But as always, the men who carried the divine seed of Yahuah disobeyed and united themselves with pagan, gentile, or nephilim-blooded women.

Through these actions, Group 2 (nephilim humans) mixed with Group 1 (Yahuah's humans) and once again corrupted the human race — Yahuah's creation — bringing us to the condition we see today.

The difference now is that those with nephilim descent — those with demon blood — have been granted a choice: whether to yield to their nephilim nature or to surrender to the divine seed of Yahuah, which was shared through the man's union.

This is the key point for understanding the truths of Scripture. Many will reject, deny, or fail to accept this truth — and that is expected. Yet those to whom Yahuah opens the eyes of understanding will finally grasp the message and the depth of the corruption that has infected humanity and Yahuah's creation.

7.4 Mixing of Lineages and Discernment by Their Fruits

What were once two clearly defined and distinct groups are no longer distinguishable. The two lineages have become mixed, appearing now as a single group within humanity.

Only the fruits — the actions — will determine who belongs to whom: to Yahuah or to the nephilim demons.

That is why Yahusha said that both groups must grow together, for they are intertwined — and only at the time of the harvest will Yahuah separate the wicked from the righteous.

Mattithyâhû (Matthew) – Chapter 13: Verses 24–30:
"He presented another parable to them, saying: The Kingdom of Heaven is like a man who sowed good seed in his field. But while men slept, his enemy came and sowed weeds among the wheat and went away. When the grass sprouted and produced grain, then the weeds also appeared. So the servants of the master of the house came and said to him, "Master, didn't you sow good seed in your field? Then where did these weeds come from?" He said to them, "An enemy has done this." The servants said to him, "Do you want us then to go and gather them up?" But he said, "No, lest while you gather up the weeds, you also uproot the wheat with them. Let both grow together until the harvest; and at the time of the harvest I will tell the reapers, 'First gather together

the weeds and bind them in bundles to burn them, but gather the wheat into my barn.'"

We often refuse to understand what the Scriptures tell us. Yahusha, our Mashiyach, clearly explains what happens and how we should act—and even more importantly, where the seed of the evil one is found.

• The Master who sows the good seed: Yahusha

• An enemy has done this: The enemy – the adversary – Mastema

• Let both grow together until the harvest: The wheat and the weeds grow together. But what does this really mean? The wicked, or servants of the Nephilim, grow alongside the servants of Yahuah. But have you ever asked yourself where? It's clear and simple: in the churches and congregations. These are filled with both the servants of Yahuah and the servants of the hosts of evil—the Nephilim descendants. We walk the same paths, follow the same teachings, and must grow together (servants of Yahuah and servants of the Nephilim). Sometimes, as Yahusha says, we can recognize them by their fruits, but only at the end of the age will we be separated on the Day of Judgment. Don't you remember that Yahusha repeatedly says, "I never knew you, workers of iniquity—into the eternal fire"? These were in the congregations, in the churches, in the groups, supposedly practicing, but not practicing the truth of Yahuah.

• Time of the harvest: The end – the final judgment

• The reapers: The angels

• Gather the weeds first (to burn them): The wicked are burned, consumed by fire.

• The wheat into my barn: The righteous in the Tabernacle or the New Jerusalem

It is of utmost importance to remember that both the wheat and the weeds are intertwined and mixed. Their roots are so similar and connected to each other that if one tries to uproot them prematurely, there's a risk of pulling up some wheat as well—and Yahuah does not desire that. We must wait until the end of time, when the angels are sent first to bind the wicked—hybrids, descendants of the Nephilim, and their followers—and burn them.

Apostle Pauls also explains this dilemma, when he presents the law of sin and death versus the law of Êlôhîym:

Rómĕos (Romans) 7:14–25:
"For we know that the law is spiritual, but I am carnal, sold under sin. For what I do, I do not understand; for what I will to do, that I do not practice; but what I hate, that I do.

If, then, I do what I will not to do, I agree with the law that it is good. But now, it is no longer I who do it, but sin that dwells in me.

For I know that in me (that is, in my flesh) nothing good dwells; for to will is present with me, but how to perform what is good I do not find.

For the good that I will to do, I do not do; but the evil I will not to do, that I practice.

Now if I do what I will not to do, it is no longer I who do it, but sin that dwells in me.

I find then a law, that evil is present with me, the one who wills to do good.

For I delight in the law of Êlôhîym according to the inward man.

But I see another law in my members, warring against the law of my mind, and bringing me into captivity to the law of sin which is in my members.

I thank Êlôhîym — through Yahusha Mâshîyach Âdônây our Master!

So then, with the mind I myself serve the law of Êlôhîym, but with the flesh the law of sin."

7.5 Qeynan – The Father of Occultism

(The man who found the writings of the Watchers and revived their forbidden wisdom.)

After the generations of Nôach (Noah) and Shem, son of Nôach, came another: the generation of Arpakshad, from whom was born a man whose existence was erased in many Bible versions — Qeynan (Cainan).

The malicious ones — or the descendants of this man — chose to erase his genealogy from Scripture so people would not know who he truly was.

However, the Book of Jubilees reveals the reason. Qeynan, son of Arpakshad, descendant of Shem and Nôach, gained access to forbidden knowledge.

When he reached adulthood and was ready to establish himself, he set out to build a city — as was the custom of men at that age. But along the way, Qeynan found a cave containing ancient writings engraved on the rock.

He read them, copied them, and hid them, saying nothing — for he knew his great-grandfather Nôach would be enraged.

Because of these teachings and writings, which Qeynan copied, preserved, and shared, he became the transmitter of forbidden knowledge.

Yôbêl (Jubilees) 8:1–3:
"In the twenty ninth jubilee, in the first week, in the beginning thereof Arpakshad took to himself a woman and her name was Râsûêyâ, the daughter of Shûshan, the daughter of Êylâm, and

she bare him a son in the third year in this week, and he called his name Qêynân. And the son grew, and his father taught him writing, and he went to seek for himself a place where he might seize for himself a city. And he found a writing which former generations had carved on the rock, and he read what was thereon, and he transcribed it and sinned owing to it; for it contained the teaching of the Watchers in accordance with which they used to observe the omens of the sun and moon and stars in all the signs of shâmayim."

This man became the father of occultism, the one who preserved the forbidden teachings of the nephilim and introduced them among the people of Yahuah — that is, among the descendants of Nôach, who had never known such practices.

Only the nephilim and their descendants in Babel possessed such knowledge before Qeynan revived it.

7.6 Abraham and Lot

(The Righteous Among the Corrupted Nations)

Several generations passed — Shelach, Êber, Péleg, Re'û, Śerûg, Nâchôr, Terach — and finally came Abraham.

Yahuah blessed His servant Abraham greatly, and his nephew Lot, his sole heir at the time, also prospered. Soon their herdsmen began to quarrel over pastureland, so Abraham and Lot decided to separate.

Abraham remained in the land of Canaan, settling in Hebron, near the oak groves of Mamre, where he built an altar to Yahuah.

Lot, however, chose the fertile plain of the Jordan, moving his tents as far as Sodom.

Berēshīṯh (Genesis) 13:10–13:
*"And Lôṭ lifted up his eyes, and beheld all the plain of Yardên,
that it was well watered everywhere, before YAHUAH destroyed
Sedôm and Ămôrâh, even as the garden of YAHUAH, like the
land of Mitsrayim, as you come unto Tsôʿar. Then Lôṭ chose
him all the plain of Yardên; and Lôṭ journeyed east: and they
separated themselves the one from the other.Abrâm dwelled in
the land of Kena'an, and Lot dwelled in the cities of the plain,
and pitched his tent toward Sedôm. But the men of Sedôm were
wicked and sinners before YAHUAH exceedingly."*

7.7 The Nephilim Kings and the War

(The Hybrid Rulers Against the Chosen of Yahuah)

It is clear that Lot settled in the region of Sodom, in the plains
of the Jordan.

Later, kings came to conquer those lands — kings from Shinar
(Babel). These rulers — descendants of the nephilim — were the
conquerors.

Berēshīṯh (Genesis) 14:1–5:
*"And it came to pass in the days of Amrâphel king of Shinʿâr,
Ăryôk king of Ellâsâr, Kedorlâʿômer king of Êylâm, and Tidʿâl
king of nations; That these made war with Bera king of Sedôm,
and with Birsha king of Ămôrâh, Shin'âb king of Admâh, and
Shem'êber king of Tsebôʿıym, and the king of Bela, which is
Tsôʿar. All these were joined together in the vale of Śıdđıym,
which is the salt sea. Twelve years they served Kedorlâʿômer,
and in the thirteenth year they rebelled. And in the fourteenth
year came Kedorlâʿômer, and the kings that were with him, and
smote the Râphâ in Ashterôth Qarnayim, and the Zûżıym in
Hâm, and the Êymıym in Shâwêh Qiryâthayim,"*

They conquered Sodom, Gomorrah, and all the neighboring cities. In that war, Lot, Abraham's nephew, was taken captive along with his possessions.

Abraham then armed his servants, pursued the invaders, and rescued his nephew, returning him to his home in Sodom — a land that had been conquered by the kings of Babel, the nephilim kings.

Remember, Shinar was the ancient name of Babel, and who were the inhabitants of Babel? As we have already established — the nephilim.

Yôbêl (Jubilees) 10:25:
"For this reason the whole land of Shinâr is called Bâbel, because Yahuah did there confound all the language of the children of men, and from thence they were dispersed into their cities, each according to his language and his nation."

Therefore, the new inhabitants of those cities — Sodom, Gomorrah, and the surrounding towns — were descendants of the nephilim. These lands were filled with their conquerors — the kings and people of Babel.

Chapter 8
Sodom and Gomorrah

*(Cities that symbolize the fullness
of sin and the justice of Yahuah)*

8.1 The Repetition of the Watchers' Sin and Their Total Destruction

As time passed, all those cities multiplied and became greatly populated — remembering that the new residents were remnants of the nephilim.

As we already know, they did not possess the "chip" of goodness or anything related to what is good. Their "chip" was destruction, war, and everything related to evil, for their nature was purely wicked.

Even though their blood was mixed with the blood of women, they were a mixed, hybrid race.

Therefore, their sin became so great that their aberration once again reached the throne of Êlôhîym, who descended to see what the inhabitants of Sodom and Gomorrah were doing. Three angels descended.

The Angel of Yahuah remained speaking with Abraham, because He knew Abraham was pure. For that reason, He did not wish to hide from him the decree that had gone forth for the destruction of Sodom and Gomorrah.

Abraham sought to intercede for the inhabitants of Sodom before Yahuah and pleaded for mercy, beginning with fifty righteous:

Berēshīṯh (Genesis) — Chapter 18: Verses 23–24:
"And Abrâhâm drew near, and said, Will you also destroy the righteous with the wicked? Peradventure there be fifty righteous

within the city: will you also destroy and not spare the place for the fifty righteous that are therein?

But there were not fifty righteous in those cities.

So Abraham reduced his plea from fifty to forty, to thirty, to twenty, and finally to ten. Among all the inhabitants of those cities there were not even ten righteous, for they were not inhabited by a pure remnant of Yahuah, but by the accursed remnants of the nephilim.

When Abraham could lower the number no further, the Angel of Yahuah departed. But the other two angels entered the city at evening and sat in the square.

Everyone saw them arrive, yet no one offered them lodging — except Lot, Abraham's nephew, who carried the "chip" of the pure, the sons of Yahuah.

Berēshīṯh (Genesis) — Chapter 19: Verse 1:
"And there came two angels to Sedôm at even; and Lôṭ sat in the gate of Sedôm: and Lôṭ seeing them rose up to meet them; and he bowed himself with his face toward the ground"

Lot offered them lodging; they did not wish to accept, but he pressed them strongly because he knew how dangerous it was for travelers to remain openly in the city.

Lot had no idea who these men were — but the descendants of the nephilim, who bore a measure of angelic nature, realized it immediately. They perceived at once that they were two angels.

Lot did not know it, but the inhabitants of the city — nephilim descendants — did. So they all came to Lot's house seeking those men.

They wanted to "know" them — that is, to lie with them, have relations, sexual intercourse — because they knew who they were.

Lot offered them his two virgin daughters, but they were not interested in virgins or in women. They were interested in repeating the great sin of their fathers: to beget a new race with angels once more.

Therefore Yahuah hastened the destruction of those inhabitants — and to be clear, this destruction fell upon the nephilim-descended inhabitants; but the humans not descended from the nephilim Yahuah rescued.

For centuries we have been taught that it was solely because of homosexuality. But if homosexuality and lesbianism have existed — sins among many others that abound among the accursed descendants of the nephilim — then there had to be something more behind those actions.

Yes — there was: to recreate the great sin of their fathers, uniting with angels to create another accursed race. But this time, Yahuah would not permit it.

This was the true reason why Yahuah destroyed not only Sodom and Gomorrah, but also all the surrounding cities.

Let us remember that only four people were rescued or spared from that entire population — and not for love of them, but for love of Abraham: Lot, his wife, and his two daughters.

Berēshīṯh (Genesis) — Chapter 19: Verse 29:
"And it came to pass, when ĔLÔHÎYM destroyed the cities of the plain, that ĔLÔHÎYM remembered Abrâhâm, and sent Lôṭ out of the midst of the overthrow, when he overthrew the cities in the which Lôṭ dwelt."

Even so, those three women carried with them the teachings of the nephilim, for they had been inhabitants of Sodom. That is why Lot's wife, when she looked back, became a pillar of salt.

Yôbêl (Jubilees) — Chapter 16: Verse 5
"And in this month Yahuah executed his judgments on Sedôm,
and Ămôrâh, and Tsebôıym, and all the region of the Yardên,
and he burned them with fire and brimstone, and destroyed them
until this day, even as lo I have declared unto you all their works,
that they are wicked and sinners exceedingly, and that they
defile themselves and commit fornication in their flesh, and work
uncleanness on the earth."

This is the description of the people of the nephilim. Let us understand what truly happened: Sodom, Gomorrah, and all the neighboring cities were destroyed because of the sin of the nephilim.

8.2 Lot and His Daughters — The Only Survivors of Sodom and Gomorrah

(The lineage of Ammon and Moab, cursed from its origin.)

Lot's daughters, who had lived within the society of the nephilim and learned their teachings, devised a plan: to intoxicate their father Lot and lie with him so as to obtain offspring.

Apparently, they did not understand that there were other human beings on the earth, and they feared being left without descendants — according to their reasoning.

But did they truly want offspring because they served Yahuah? Or because they had learned the evil practices of the nephilim? (Reflective thought.)

The first night, they made their father drunk, and one of them lay with him. They repeated the act the second night. But what kind of drunkenness was this, in which Lot apparently did not realize it, according to the account in Berēšhīth? (Reflective thought.)

One daughter bore Ammon, and the other Moab. These were the sons of that aberrant union between the daughters and their father.

Apparently, this would be the end of the story — but it is not. The truth of this account has been hidden, yet no hidden truth fails to come to light.

The Book of Jubilees tells us that Yahuah cursed the descendants of that union because Lot lay with his daughters. It is obvious that Lot knew what he had done. We should not pretend or think that Lot did not realize or did not remember what happened.

Therefore Yahuah cursed him and declared the destiny of Lot and his descendants forever:

Yôbêl (Jubilees) — Chapter 16: Verses 8–9
"And he and his daughters committed sin upon the earth, such as had not been on the earth since the days of Âdâm till his time; for the man lay with his daughters. And, behold, it was commanded and engraven concerning all his seed, on the shâmayim tablets, to remove them and root them out, and to execute judgment upon them like the judgment of Sedôm, and to leave no seed of the man on earth on the day of condemnation."

To the sons of this union — Ammon (Ammonites) and Moab (Moabites) — it was decreed that they would be completely uprooted from the face of the earth, together with all their descendants. Not one will remain on the earth from this line on the day of final judgment; all will be completely exterminated.

Tsephanyâhû (Zephaniah) — Chapter 2: Verse 9
"Therefore as I live, says YAHUAH Tsâbâ, the ĔLÔHÎYM of Yâshârêl, surely Môâb shall be as Sedôm, and the children of Ammôn as Ămôrâh, even the breeding of nettles, and salt pits, and a perpetual desolation: the residue of my people shall spoil them, and the remnant of my people shall possess them."

(Moab is called Jordan today, and Ammon extended its borders westward to the Jordan River, north to Gilead, and south to Heshbon, between the Syrian desert and the Jordan River, and between the Jabbok and Arnon rivers — in present-day Jordan. In the Persian period, the term "Ammonite" had become merely geographic, applied especially to the Arab tribes that had settled in the territory of the ancient kingdom of Ammon. Milcom (perhaps a variation of Moloch) was the principal deity, while El, Baal, and the moon deity were also prominent gods.)

8.3 The Legacy of the Watchers

(The secrets transmitted by the fallen ones that still govern humanity)

8.3.1 Teachings of the Watcher Angels

(The revealed mysteries that corrupted the earth)

It has always been said that the downfall of humanity came from the forbidden teachings that the Watcher angels imparted to their women, and that these women, in turn, taught to their children — thus spreading throughout society.

To better understand the ramifications of these teachings, let us remember what is written:

> *Chănôk (Enoch) — Chapter 10: Verse 7*
> *"And heal the earth which the angels have corrupted, and proclaim the healing of the earth, that they may heal the plague, and that all the children of men may not perish through all the secret things that the Watchers have disclosed and have taught their sons."*

This mystery, which so fascinates humanity, is the cause of its destruction. It is natural that it would fascinate the descendants of the nephilim, for these teachings are their own; whereas, for the sons of Yahuah, they are nothing but demonic doctrines.

Chănôk (Enoch) — Chapter 16: Verse 3

"You have been in shâmayim, but all the mysteries had not yet been revealed to you, and you knew worthless ones, and these in the hardness of your hearts you have made known to the women, and through these mysteries women and
men work much evil on earth."

The Watchers who descended upon the earth revealed to humans what was secret and led them into sin.

To this is added the great fault of Qeynan, who transmitted the teachings of the Watchers to humanity, becoming the father of occultism.

Knowing that Babel is the cradle of the descendants of the nephilim, it is well established that all hidden, forbidden, and demonic teachings proceed from them. But what are those teachings?

Chapter 9
Teachings of the Watchers

(The mysteries revealed by the fallen: magic, war, the heavens, and the root of human occultism)

9.1 Magic, Weapons, Cosmology, and the Hidden Origin of All Forbidden Knowledge

Chănôk (Enoch) — Chapter 7: Verse 1
"And all the others together with them took unto themselves women, and each chose for himself one, and they began to go in unto them and to defile themselves with them, and they taught them charms and enchantments, and the cutting of roots, and made them acquainted with plants."

9.1.2 Witchcraft (spells)

Witchcraft is the body of beliefs, practical knowledge, and activities attributed to certain persons called witches or sorcerers, who are thought to possess magical abilities.

Though many are unfamiliar with the term, farmakía belongs to this same class or practice of the nephilim: the ancient pharmaceutical/poisoning craft of witches or sorceresses.

Apokálypsis (Revelation) — Chapter 9: Verse 21
"They repented neither of their murders, nor of their farmakía, nor of their idolatry, nor of their thefts."

9.1.3 Magic (enchantments)

Magic, understood as an occult art or science, consists of beliefs and practices that seek to produce supernatural results through rituals, spells, and invocations.

The term "magic" is also used for the art of illusion (stage magic), which uses techniques or tricks to create illusions in entertainment — but this is distinct from the occult practices referenced here.

9.1.4 Cutting of roots and the use of plants

This refers specifically to the negative connotation — that is, instructions to use plants for evil: in witchcraft, sorcery, magic, and related arts (potions, brews, and noxious concoctions). This does not include the medicinal use of plants as guided by Yahuah.

The branch of farmakía is formed by these three primordial nephilim practices.

Apokálypsis (Revelation) — Chapter 18: Verse 23
"And the light of a candle shall shine no more at all in you; and the voice of the bridegroom and of the bride shall be heard no more at all in you: for your merchants were the great men of the earth; for by your farmakía were all nations deceived."

9.2 Drinking Blood

This is one of the favorite practices of the nephilim and their descendants, which has passed down to our generations and still prevails today — often without our noticing. Drinking blood is the same as eating blood.

Wayyīqrā (Leviticus) — Chapter 17: Verse 14
"For it is the life of all flesh; the blood of it is for the life thereof:

therefore I said unto the children of Yâshârêl, You shall eat the blood of no manner of flesh: for the life of all flesh is the blood thereof: whosoever eats it shall be cut off."

Debārīm (Deuteronomy) — Chapter 12: Verse 23
"Only be sure that you eat not the blood: for the blood is the life; and you may not eat the life with the flesh."

Prásso (Acts) — Chapter 15: Verse 29
"That you abstain from food offered to idols, and from blood, and from things strangled, and from pornia: from which if you keep yourselves, you shall do well. Farewell."

Chănôk (Enoch) — Chapter 7: Verse 5
"And they began to sin against birds, and beasts, and reptiles, and fish, and to devour one another's flesh, and drink the blood."

In my country, the Dominican Republic, there is a common practice that many enjoy called morcillas — sausage prepared with animal intestines filled with the animal's blood. This practice has many names depending on the country:

• Latin America: Moronga (Mexico, Nicaragua, El Salvador, Guatemala, Honduras), Sangrecita (Peru), Prieta (Chile), Rellena (various).

• Spain: Morcilla (most common; regional varieties include Burgos, León, Palencia, Beasain), Fariñón/Fariñona (Asturias), Emberzao/ Pantrucu (Asturias).

• Other countries: Blutwurst (Germany, Austria), Morcilla de Colonia/Flönz (Rhineland, Germany), Soondae (Korea), Dinuguan (Philippines).

9.3 Asael (Azazel) and the Technology of War and Vanity

Chǎnôk (Enoch) — Chapter 8: Verse 1

"And Ăzâzêl taught men to make swords, and knives, and shields, and breastplates, and made known to them the metals of the earth and the art of working them, and bracelets, and ornaments, and the use of antimony, and the beautifying of the eyelids, and all kinds of costly stones, and all coloring tinctures."

All injustice upon the earth revealing eternal secrets fulfilled on heaven — and all began to disclose secrets to their wives. Among the teachings:

• Forging iron swords — instruments of war and death.

• Copper breastplates — instruments of protection in war.

• Gold and silver in bracelets and ornaments — superfluous adornment and vanity.

• Antimony for women — historically used in cosmetics to line the eyes and brows.

• Eye makeup.

• Precious stones.

• Dyes and tinctures.

(You may consult reference links regarding the modern evolution of these practices; bear in mind that most sources do not know their true origin — the nephilim.)

9.4 Other Watchers and Their Nephilim Teachings

Chănôk (Enoch) — Chapter 8: Verse 3
"Semyaza taught enchantments, and root cuttings, Armaros the resolving of enchantments, Baraqiyal taught astrology, Kokhebel the constellations, Ezeqeel the knowledge of the clouds, Araqiel the signs of the earth, Shamsiel the signs of the sun, and Sariel the course of the moon."

• Shemihaza — enchantments and root-cutting.

• Hermoni (Amaros) — breaking spells; practicing witchcraft, magic, and related skills (no matter the modern names, the diabolic origin remains).

• Baraqel — the signs of lightning (astronomy).

• Kokabel — the omens of the stars (constellations: astronomy and astrology).

• Zeqel — lightnings and their meanings (cloud lore: astronomy/astrology).

• Artaqof (Araqi-el) — signs of the earth (geodesy, topography).

• Shamsiel — omens of the sun (astrology; solar physics/heliophysics).

• Sahariel — of the moon (astrology; selenography).

Chănôk (Enoch) — Chapter 9: Verse 6
"You see what Ăzâzêl has done, who has taught all unrighteousness on earth and revealed the eternal secrets which were preserved in shâmayim, which men were striving to learn:"

Chănôk (Enoch) — Chapter 19: Verse 1
"And Ûrîyêl said to me: Here shall stand the angels who have

connected themselves with women, and their spirits assuming many different forms are defiling mankind and shall lead them astray into sacrificing to demons as gods, here they shall stand, till the day of the great judgement in which they shall be judged till they are made an end of."

To sacrifice to demons as gods is exactly where we find ourselves today, though many cannot see or accept it — a chief nephilim practice to drag as many as possible into perdition.

Chănôk (Enoch) — Chapter 69: Verses 8 & 12
"And the fourth was named Penemuel: He taught the children of men the bitter and the sweet, and he taught them all the secrets of their wisdom. And the fifth was named Kasdeya: This is he who showed the children of men all the wicked smitings of spirits and demons, and the smitings of the embryo in the womb, that it may pass away, and the smitings of the soul the bites of the serpent, and the smitings which befall through the noontide heat, the son of the serpent named Tabaêt."

• The bitter and the sweet: Evil's sweetness quickly fades, but its bitterness remains; it feigns life but steals it, enchanting the senses while corroding the spirit.

• Writing with ink and paper: Evil writes like dark ink upon a pure page; at first the stain seems small, but it spreads, covering the page's purpose, rewriting truth with lies. Only the Word of Yahuah can cleanse the page and restore its light.

• Evil attacks of demons: Malignant spiritual manifestations that seek to oppress, deceive, and divert the believer through fear, temptations, and afflictions of soul and body.

• Attacks on the embryo (abortion): One of the darkest corruptions taught by the Watchers — the destruction of life before birth — rebellion against the sacred gift of Yahuah, extinguishing a light before its time and turning the womb — designed for life — into a place of death.

• Attacks on the soul: Invisible aggressions that aim to break faith, hope, and spiritual identity, working through guilt, fear, and confusion to sever one's connection with Yahuah and plant inner emptiness where peace and truth once dwelt.

And some still ask about the origin of abortion — it is plainly a nephilim teaching used to destroy humanity, Yahuah's creation. Reading carefully, we discern the enemy's tactics and practices to destroy the people of Yahuah.

9.5 Summary of Main Nephilim Practices

Below is a list of main nephilim practices to review and study as needed. Remember: this list presents the essentials — not all historical variations, names, or branches that the nephilim have created to confuse humanity.

• Witchcraft / Sorcery / Magic (enchantments, spells, invocations)

• Farmakía (potions, drugs, ritual preparations)

• Astrology / Omen-reading (sun, moon, constellations, lightning, clouds)

• Warfare metallurgy (swords, shields, breastplates) and vanity (adornments, cosmetics)

• Consumption of blood and corruption of creatures (hybridizations)

Yôbêl (Jubilees) — Chapter 12: Verses 16–20
"And in the sixth week, in the fifth year thereof, Abrâm sat up throughout the night on the beginning of the seventh month to observe the stars from the evening to the morning, in order to see what would be the character of the year with regard to the rains, and he was alone as he sat and observed. And a word came

into his heart and he said: *All the signs of the stars, and the signs of the moon and of the sun are all in the hand of Yahuah. Why do I search them out? If he desires, he causes it to rain, morning and evening; and if he desires, he withholds it, and all things are in his hand.And he prayed that night and said, my Êlôhîym, Êlôhîym Elyôn Êl, you alone are my Êlôhîym, and you and your dominion I have chosen. And you have created all things, and all things that are the work of your hands.Deliver me from the hands of evil spirits who have dominion over the thoughts of men's hearts, and do not let them lead me astray from you, my Êlôhîym. And you establish me and my seed forever that we do not go astray from henceforth and forevermore."*

What Abraham did might seem innocent — observing the stars to forecast the year's rains — but if it were harmless, why was he reproved? The practice of watching the stars and constellations to predict whether there will be rain, storms, or anything else is not pleasing to Yahuah; it is the practice of the Nephilim.

When Abraham understood his error, he prayed and repented, giving us something powerful: "Deliver me from the hands of the evil spirits who rule the thoughts of human hearts."

This is what we call malignant influences swarming the thoughts of people — even of Yahuah's children. This is the sum of what evil spirits can do. Our work, then, is to plead with Yahuah to deliver us from such influences and thoughts.

Chănôk (Enoch) — Chapter 54: Verses 6
"... that Yahuah of Rûach may take vengeance on them for their unrighteousness in becoming subject to the adversary and leading astray those who dwell on the earth."

Demons — the nephilim — and their teachings lead humanity to perdition. Whether or not we accept it, Yahuah will avenge

Himself on them for serving as instruments of the adversary and for leading humans astray. This is biblical truth.

9.6 The Nephilim in Scripture

(Direct biblical references to their existence)

Berēshīṯh (Genesis) 6:4
"There were Nephîyl in the earth in those days; and also after that, when the sons of ĔLÔHÎYM came in unto the daughters of men, and they bare children to them, the same became mighty men which were of old, men of renown."

This is the first mention in Bereshith of the existence of the Nephilim (or Nephiyl), and as you can see, it clearly states that they mingled with women and produced mighty men — in other words, exactly what we have been saying from the beginning: the giants, or Nephilim.

9.7 The Nephilim in the Promised Land

(Giants who inhabited Canaan)

Môsheh sent men to spy out the land, and the scouts reached the land of Chebrón (Hebron), inhabited by:

Bemīḏbar (Numbers) 13:22
"And they ascended by the south, and came unto Chebrôn; where Ăchîyman, Shêshay, and Talmay, the children of Ânâq, were. (Now Chebrôn was built seven years before Tsôan in Mitsrayim.)"

At Hebron were Ăchîyman, Shêshay, and Talmay — nephilim — sons of Ânâq (Watcher angels). Hebron was built seven years before Tsôan of Mitsrayim (Egypt), indicating that Tsôan in Egypt is also of nephilim origin.

Bemīḏbar (Numbers) 13:33
"And there we saw the nephîyl, the sons of Ânâq, which come of the nephîyl: and we were in our own sight as grasshoppers, and so we were in their sight."

Thus, the giants/Nephîyl (nephilim) are the sons of Ânâq (Watcher angels).

9.8 The Sons of Ânâq

(Direct descendants of the Watchers)

Debārīm (Deuteronomy) 9:2
"A people great and tall, the children of the Ănâĝîy, whom you know, and of whom you have heard say, Who can stand before the children of Ânâq!"

Ănâĝîy is the gentilic of Ânâq — descendants of the Watcher angels, known in the world as the Annunaqiy.

9.9 Kâlêb and the Sons of Ânâq

(The expulsion of the giants by the faith of the righteous)

Yahusha (Joshua) 15:13
"And unto Kâlêb the son of Yephûnneh he gave a part among the children of Yahûdâh, according to the commandment of YAHUAH to Yahusha, even the city of Arba the father of Ânâq, which city is Chebrôn."

Arba (Qiryath-Arba) is the father of the Ânâq, who were in Hebron; therefore Arba is a nephilim-descended ruler. From him come the Anaqiy/Anaq, also known historically as the Annunaqiy.

Kâlêb drove out the three sons of Ânâq — the giant descendants of the nephilim — who lived in Arba (Hebron), in the hill country of Yahudah. Scripture clearly tells us who the nephilim are, where they settled, and which cities they ruled; yet many refuse to see the truth — for admitting it would mean acknowledging long-held blindness or error.

9.10 The Râphâ, Zûzîym, and Êymîym

(Hybrid remnants among neighboring nations)

Berēšhīṯh (Genesis) 14:5
"And in the fourteenth year came Kedorlâ ômer, and the kings that were with him, and smote the Râphâ in Ashterôth Qarnayim, and the Zûzıym in Hâm, and the Êymıym in Shâwêh Qiryâthayim,"

Râphâ, Zûzîym, and Êymîym are different names for remnants of the nephilim/giants.

Debārīm (Deuteronomy) 2:10–11
"The Êymıym dwelt therein in times past, a people great, and many, and tall, as the Ănâq̇ıy;Which also were accounted Râphâ, as the Ănâq̇ıy; but the Môâb called them Êymıym."

Debārīm (Deuteronomy) 2:20
"That also was accounted a land of Râphâ: Râphâ dwelt therein in old time; and the Ammôn̈ıy call them Zamzôm;"

9.11 Og of Bâshân — Last Giant King

(The last bastion of the nephilim on earth)

Debārīm (Deuteronomy) 3:10
*"All the cities of the plain, and all Gilâd, and all Bâshân, unto
Salkâh and Edrêiy, cities of the kingdom of Ôg in Bâshân."*

Og of Bashan was one of the last giant nephilim kings.

Debārīm (Deuteronomy) 3:13
*"And the rest of Gilâd, and all Bâshân, being the kingdom of Ôg,
gave I unto the half tribe of Menashsheh; all the region of Argôb,
with all Bâshân, which was called the land of Râphâ."*

Bashan is also known as the land of the giant nephilim. Do we not yet see it? Land of the giants — that is, of the nephilim.

Chapter 10
Giants in the Days of Dâwid

(The final war between the servants of Yahuah and the descendants of the giants)

10.1 Golyath of Gath

1 Shemûêl (1 Samuel) 17:4
"And there went out a champion out of the camp of the Pelishtiy, named Golyath, of Gath, whose height was six cubits and a span."

The giant Golyath was a descendant of the nephilim. Remember that the Philistines are associated with nephilim; that is why we see that many of the giants arise from among the Philistines.

Berēšhīṯh (Genesis) — Chapter 10: Verse 14
** And Pathrûsıy, and Kaslûchıym, and the Chasmoniym (out of whom came Pelishtıy, and Kaphtôrıy."

We thus see that the fathers of the Philistines are the "Chasmoniyn" (Hasmoneans/Asmoneans). Therefore, these progenitors are presented as the forebears of the nephilim dwelling among the Philistines.

10.2 Other Giants Fallen by Dâwid and His Servants

2 Shemûêl (2 Samuel) 21:16–17
"And Yishbô Benôb, which was of the sons of the râphâ, the weight of whose spear weighed three hundred shekels of brass in weight, he being girded with a new sword, thought to have slain Dâwid. But Ăbıyshay the son of Tserûyâh succoured him,

and smote the Pelishtıy, and killed him. Then the men of Dâwid
swore unto him, saying, you shall go no more out with us to
battle, that you quench not the light of Yâshârêl."

Yishbô Benôb, a son of the giant Râphâ, died at the hand of Ăbîyshay.

2 Shemûêl (2 Samuel) 21:18–22
"And it came to pass after this, that there was again a battle with
the Pelishtıy at Gôb: then Sibbekay the Chûshâthıy slew Saph,
which was of the sons of the râphâ. And there was again a battle
in Gôb with the Pelishtıy, where Elchânân the son of Yaărêy
Ôreĝıym, a Bêyth Hallachmîy, slew the brother of Golyath the
Gitlıy, the staff of whose spear was like a weaver's beam. And
there was yet a battle in Gath, where was a man of great stature,
that had on every hand six fingers, and on every foot six toes,
four and twenty in number; and he also was born to the râphâ.
And when he defied Yâshârêl, Yahônâthân the son of Shimâ the
brother of Dâwid slew him.These four were born to the râphâ
in Gath, and fell by the hand of Dâwid, and by the hand of his
servants."

Thus Dâwid and his men struck down four giants born to Râphâ.

10.3 Nephilim Presence Throughout the Scriptures

As we can see, the nephilim — the giants — appear throughout the Scriptures. Though some novices may claim they were merely tall humans, the Scriptures are clear: they were giants, and if you read carefully, you see they are the descendants of the nephilim.

I understand that many evade these truths, unwilling to accept them — for it would mean admitting ignorance or error, and, worse, it would tear away the veil of lies that has long been used to keep us from recognizing, all around us, the sons of darkness — the offspring of demons.

We can trace nephilim presence through all biblical history — from Nôach, the patriarchs, the judges, the kings, the prophets — down to our own time. To catalog all their deeds would require volumes; here are but a few references.

10.4 Worship of Baal (Prophets and Kings Who Confronted It)

1. Gid'on (Gideon) — Idol: Baal, Asherah

Scripture: Shophetim / Judges 6:25–32
Summary: Destroyed his father's altar to Baal and cut down the Asherah pole, reestablishing worship to Yahuah.

2. Achâb (Ahab) & Îyzebel (Jezebel) — Idol: Baal, Asherah

Scripture: 1 Melakim / 1 Kings 16:31–33
Summary: Introduced Phoenician Baal-worship in Yâshârêl; built a temple for Baal in Shomrón (Samaria).

3. Êlîyâhû (Elijah) — Idol: Baal

Scripture: 1 Melakim / 1 Kings 18:17–40
Summary: Challenged 450 prophets of Baal on Mount Karmel; Yahuah answered by fire, proving His supremacy.

4. Êlîyshâ / Yêhû (Elisha / Jehu) — Idol: Baal

Scripture: 2 Melakim / 2 Kings 10:18–28
Summary: Yehu destroyed Baal's temple and priests, fulfilling Yahuah's judgment declared by Eliyahu.

5. Hoshea (Hosea) — Idol: Baal, Ashtarot

Scripture: Hoshea 2:8–13; 13:1–2
Summary: Condemned Yâshârêl for spiritual adultery in pursuing the Baalim.

6. YirmeYahu (Jeremiah) — Idol: Baal

Scripture: YirmeYahu 2:8; 19:5; 32:35
Summary: Denounced Yahudah (Judah) for burning incense to Baal and sacrificing children to Molek.

7. TsefanYahu (Zephaniah) — Idol: Baal

Scripture: TsefanYahu 1:4–6
Summary: Prophesied that Yahuah would remove the name of Baal from Yahudah.

10.5 Asherah / Queen of Heaven

• Shelomoh (Solomon) — Idol: Ashtoreth (ʿAŠtōret)

Scripture: 1 Melakim / 1 Kings 11:4–8

Summary: Built high places for Ashtoreth and Kemosh under the influence of foreign wives.

• YirmeYahu (Jeremiah) — Idol: Queen of Heaven (Ishtar/Astarte)

Scripture: YirmeYahu 7:18; 44:17–19

Summary: Condemned the people for baking cakes and burning incense to the Queen of Heaven.

- **Mikhah (Micah)** — Idol: Asherah and carved images

Scripture: Mikhah 1:6–7; 5:13

Summary: Prophesied that Yahuah would destroy all idols and sacred poles.

10.6 Molek / Child Sacrifice (Tophet in the Valley of Hinnom)

- Achâz (Ahaz) — Idol: Molek (Mōleḵ)

Scripture: 2 Melakim / 2 Kings 16:3–4

Summary: Caused his son to pass through the fire, imitating the abominations of the Kenaʿanim (Canaanites).

- Menashsheh (Manasseh) — Idols: Molek, Baal

Scripture: 2 Melakim / 2 Kings 21:3–7

Summary: Rebuilt altars to Baal, raised an Asherah pole, and offered his sons in fire.

- YirmeYahu (Jeremiah) — Idol: Molek

Scripture: YirmeYahu 7:31; 19:5; 32:35

Summary: Condemned the sacrifice of sons and daughters in Topheth (Valley of Hinnom).

10.7 Golden Calves and False Centers of Worship

- Aharon / Yâshârêl — Idol: Golden Calf

Scripture: Shemoth / Exodus 32:1–35

Summary: Yâshârêl worshiped a golden calf at Sinai, calling it their god; Yahuah's anger burned against them.

• Yerov ʿam (Jeroboam) — Idols: Golden Calves

Scripture: 1 Melakim / 1 Kings 12:28–33

Summary: Set up calves at Beit-El and Dan to keep the people from Yerushalayim: "These are your gods, O Yâshârêl!"

• Chizqiyahu (Hezekiah) — Idol: Nehushtan (bronze serpent)

Scripture: 2 Melakim / 2 Kings 18:4

Summary: Destroyed the bronze serpent when people began burning incense to it.

10.8 Worship of the Sun, the Stars, and the "Host of the Heavens"

• Menashsheh (Manasseh) — Idol: Host of Heaven

Scripture: 2 Melakim / 2 Kings 21:3–5

Summary: Built altars to celestial bodies inside the Temple and worshiped the host of the shâmayim.

• Yechezqê'l (Ezekiel) — Vision 1 — Idol: Image of Jealousy

Scripture: Yechezqê'l 8:5–6

Summary: A provocative image near the north gate that provoked Yahuah to jealousy.

• Yechezqê'l — Vision 2 — Idol: Engravings and creeping things

Scripture: Yechezqê'l 8:10–12

Summary: Seventy elders burning incense before engraved

abominations on the Temple walls.

• Yechezqê'l — Vision 3 (Explicit) — Idol: Women weeping for Tammûz (Tammuz)

Scripture: Yechezqê'l 8:14

Summary: Women at the north gate of Yahuah's house weeping for Tammuz.

• Yechezqê'l — Vision 4 — Idol: Sun worship

Scripture: Yechezqê'l 8:16–18

Summary: Twenty-five men worshiping the sun toward the east inside the inner court.

• Amos — Idols: Sikkuth, Kiyun

Scripture: Amos 5:25–27

Summary: Condemned Yâshârêl for carrying images of astral deities alongside the worship of Yahuah.

10.9 Babylonian Idols (Bel, Nebo, Dragon)

• YashaYahu (Isaiah) — Idols: Bel, Nebo

Scripture: YashaYahu 46:1–2

Summary: Mocked the Babylonian gods that must be carried by men and cannot save themselves.

• Dânîyêl — Bel and the Dragon 1:1–28 — Idols: Bel, Dragon

Summary: Proved that Bel (baal) was a fraud and destroyed the idol dragon, showing idols have no power.

10.10 Final Meditation

L et us ponder this brief list and see how the nephilim have always been there — stumbling blocks, infiltrating the things of Yahuah. The notion sold to us — that the nephilim and their descendants are matters of the past — has been carefully constructed so that we would believe it. But the reality is more striking — even terrifying — than it appears.

The nephilim and their descendants are among us, much closer than we think. By the end of these writings, we will either see clearly — or remain totally blind.

Chapter 11
Remnant of the Nephilim in New Testament Times

(The infiltration of the accursed lineage in the apostolic era)

11.1 The Visible Traces of the Nephilim in Scripture

These are the most visible traces found in Scripture about the nephilim giants or the remnant of the nephilim.

However, we must also consider other factors to better understand the magnitude of this accursed race.

Hidden factors that broaden our understanding of the accursed race

Let us analyze one specific verse to begin disproving the false narratives about the race or descendants of the nephilim.

We are clear that Babel is the cradle of the nephilim and that they were dispersed among all nations, tribes, peoples, and tongues. But let us begin this journey with something ancient and unusual.

The enigma of Genesis 10:14

Genesis 10:14 — "and the Patrosim, and the Chasmoniim (from whom came the Phylistiim), and the Gaphthoriim." (Brenton's Septuagint Translation).

Berēshīṯh (Genesis) — Chapter 10: Verse 14: And the Pathrûsîy (יסְרְתֿפ), and the Kaslûchîym and the Chasmoniym, from whom came the Pelishtîy, and the Kaphtôrîy.

The descendants of Châm (Ham) and the mixing with nephilim

blood

All of these come from the line of Châm (Ham), settled in the region of Canaan — those who mixed with nephilim blood, creating the generation we recognize to this day.

The textual difference in the Septuagint

As you can see, the Septuagint preserves a difference in the text: it has "Chasmoniin." Now, among the groups presented in Berēšhīth, there are four: Pathrûsîy, Kaslûchîym (from whom came the Pelishtîy/Philistines), and Kaphtôrîy (Gath/Caphtor).

If you carefully study the division of the land in the days of Nôach, you will notice that each of these groups are descendants or peoples inhabited by nephilim, including the Philistines and Gath/Caphtor, from whom the giants arise.

"Chasmoniin": the hidden clue and erased name of the Philistines

However, the Septuagint gives us an additional clue—"Chasmoniin," known as the "Asmoneans/Hasmoneans," who are the same people as the Philistines, only under a different name. The name "Asmoneans" has been concealed for centuries for many reasons; and to bring this name to light, a false narrative around the books of the Maccabees was crafted in the period between Malachi and Matthew (New Testament).

Initial revelatory summary

Summarizing and emphasizing for clarity to start with: Babel, cradle of the nephilim, was scattered everywhere; Kasluchiyn, a group of nephilim from whom came the Pelishtiy (Philistines), who carry the same hidden name "Hasmoneans/Asmoneans." This leads us to a nephilim demon mentioned in the Book of Tobit. This nephilim is cast out and then dwells in Egypt, where he makes his new abode.

Asmodeus: the revealed nephilim demon

Asmodeus (Hebrew: אַשְׁמְדּאָי, 'Ašməddāy; ancient Greek:

Ἀσμοδαῖος, Asmodaios) — also called Asmodeus, Asmodaios, Asmodai, Hasmoday, Chashmodai, Azmonden, Sidonay — is one of the princes of demons in the demonology of the Abrahamic religions.

Asmodeus/Chasmodai comes from aēšma-daēva (cf. aeshma/hashem/hashema), which correlates with Chasmoniyn/Asmoneans.

11.2 The Gods of the Nations and the Nephilim Connection

Melāḵīm (2 Kings) — Chapter 17: Verses 29–31
"Howbeit every nation made gods of their own, and put them in
the houses of the high places which the Shômerôñıy had made,
every nation in their cities wherein they dwelt. And the men of
Bâbel made Sûkkôth Benôth, and the men of Kûth made Nêrgal,
and the men of Chămâth made Ăshıymâ, And the Awwiym
made Nibchaz and Tartâq, and the Sepharwîıy burnt their
children in fire to Adrammelek and Ânammelek, the gods of
Sepharwayim."

Ashima / Aeshema / Asmodeus: the god of the Samaritans

This is the Samaritans' god — Ashima/Aeshema/Asmodeus — the same father-figure of the Philistines/Asmoneans/Chasmoniym.

Did you know the Samaritans were inhabitants of Cainan, as their land was called? And do you know what Cainan really is? Cainan/Canaan is the descendant of the father of occultism, "Qeynan," the very one who found the hidden teachings of the nephilim, copied them, learned them, and spread them. Do you understand?

The Asmoneans: usurpers of the Temple and heirs of the fallen lineage

Around 120 BC, the Chamonean/Asmonean revolt took place; they usurped the Temple, replaced the High Priest, and remained as the supposed representatives of the Temple. They held total power, and these are the same ones who continued in leadership in the days of Constantine, and are tied to the leadership of the Roman Empire that shapes our world today.

This raises the question: why do the terms Pharisees, Sadducees, Essenes do not appear in the Old Testament, but only in the New? These factional groups, all belonging to the same movement/ lineage connected with the nephilim, had taken complete control of the Temple and of everything religious.

The Wicked Priest and the profanation of the Day of Atonement

"Moreover, wine is treacherous; the arrogant man is never at rest."

Our commentator reads bôn ("wealth") instead of hayyayin ("wine") and explains that the passage refers to the Wicked Priest, whose heart was exalted upon gaining power, so that he abandoned God and acted treacherously against the ordinances for the sake of wealth (1QpHab viii 10ff.).

"The Wicked Priest pursued the Teacher of Righteousness to destroy him in his hot fury, even to the point of being discovered," F. F. Bruce, "The Habakkuk Scroll of Qumran," Annual of the Leeds University Oriental Society I (1958/59): 5–24.

On the holy day of rest — the Day of Atonement — he burst in among them to devour them and make them stumble on the fast day, their Sabbath of rest.

Thus ran the religious reign of the Asmoneans, progenitors linked with the Philistines, ancestrally hidden so that we would not know that their nephilim descendants are the Pharisees, Sadducees, and Essenes in the time of Yahusha Ha Mashiyach.

11.3 Yahusha and the Confrontation with the Nephilim Lineage

(The lineage of rebellion before the Son of Man.)

Yahusha Ha Mashiyach encounters this context when He comes to His people. Yahusha is completely clear in telling us who they are and what their lineage is — He says they are "children of demons."

If that wording is unfamiliar, consider His phrase "children of your father the devil." Or, if you prefer, "children of the nephilim." Choose whichever term is clearer — they refer to the same groups in Yahusha's day, which is our New Testament starting point.

To be clear: Pharisees, Sadducees, and Essenes are servants and sons of the Chasmoniim, the fathers of the Philistines, who in turn are the nephilim lineage. Nephilim, Ishmaelites, Edomites, Asmoneans (Chasmoneans), Pharisees, Essenes, Sadducees, Constantine (Roman Empire) — all serving and following the line of their progenitor: Babel/nephilim.

11.4 Yôchânân the Baptistis (John the Baptist) — Denunciation of the Nephilim

(The Pharisees, the Sadducees, and the generation of Echidna)

Mattithyâhû (Matthew) — Chapter 3: Verse 7
"But when he saw many of the Pârâsh and Tsâdôq come to his baptism, he said unto them, O generation of Echidna, who has warned you to flee from the wrath to come?"

In traditional translations you find "brood of vipers," but the Greek term is ἔχιδνα (echidna). A simple search shows that Echidna, in Greek mythology, is a monstrous female of the serpentine line (one of the Phorcydes).

For those who still do not grasp it: Yôchânân knows who they are, whom they serve, and what their genealogy is. Echidna is a female demon; translating it simply as "viper" obscures the original meaning.

If Yôchânân calls them a generation of echidna = demons, what part do we not understand? And to whom does he say this? To the Pârâsh and Tsâdôq — that is, Pharisees and Sadducees — the leaders after the usurpation of the Temple. But perhaps it is still not clear because, you might say, "Yahusha didn't say that." Did He?

11.5 Yahusha Ha Mashiyach Faces the Nephilim

Mattithyâhû (Matthew) — Chapter 12: Verse 34
"O generation of Echidna, how can you, being evil, speak good things? For out of the abundance of the heart the mouth speaks."

Mattithyâhû (Matthew) — Chapter 23: Verse 33
"You serpents, you generation of Echidna, how can you escape the damnation of geenna?"

Who is speaking, and to whom? Reading the context shows it is Yahusha Himself who calls the Pharisees and Sadducees a generation of echidna — a generation of demons — which, to clarify, is the same as a generation of nephilim.

The role of this generation of demons from the beginning has been to oppose everything related to Yahuah, persecute His followers, and kill Yahuah's prophets. And what do they do with Yahusha? This generation of echidna seeks to kill Him, attempting it several times, though His hour had not yet come.

In the crowds during Yahusha's preaching and teaching there were always two main groups:

1. Those who genuinely wanted to hear Yahusha and know Yahuah.

2. Those who opposed everything Yahusha said — the religious leaders who had usurped the Temple, changed the High Priest, and instituted their own religion, not Yahuah's, but that of their ancestors/progenitors — the nephilim.

Pay close attention to Yahusha's words: He first addresses the needy people who hungers for truth, and then He addresses the children/descendants of demons — echidna — nephilim (use whichever term you better understand).

Mattithyâhû (Matthew) — Chapter 16: Verse 4
"A wicked and adulterous generation seeks after a sign; and there shall no sign be given unto it, but the sign of the prophet Yônâh. And he left them, and departed."

Yôchânân (John) — Chapter 8: Verse 44
"You are of your father the diabolos, and the lusts of your father you will do. He was a murderer from the beginning, and did not stay in the truth, because there is no truth in him. When he speaks a lie, he speaks of his own: for he is a liar, and the father of it."

These are just a few verses; all Scripture is filled with references to these groups, consistently refuting, denying, and attempting to discredit Yahusha's truth with the lies of their father. If Yahusha calls them "children of the devil" — that is, children of a demon — then if their father is the devil, what would they be?

11.6 Maśṭêmâh in the New Testament

The temptation of Yahusha, where the adversary comes and tempts Him using Scripture. This tempter was not merely a demon or a nephilim; this tempter is the same angel we see in the Old Testament, testing the followers of Yahuah.

In some places you see satan, but remember the word is not a proper name — it means adversary, enemy, opposer. This is why you see Yahusha converse with this angel and, without uttering a curse, simply answers with the truth of the Word.

Mattithyâhû (Matthew) — Chapter 4: Verse 3
'And when the tempter came to him, he said, if you are the son of

Êlôhîym, command that these stones be made bread."

Mattithyâhû (Matthew) — Chapter 4: Verse 11
"Then the Diabolos left him, and, behold, angels came and ministered unto him."

Διάβολος (diabolos): a slanderer, (compare [H7854]): false accuser, devil, slanderer.

This is the Greek word to understand when Yahusha rebukes the diabolos and he departs — in other words, He rebukes the slanderer, tempter, accuser.

But this Greek term traces to the Hebrew H7854, śâțân (שָׂטָן) — an opponent, adversary, one who resists — the very figure we mentioned in the Old Testament by the proper name "Maśțêmâh." He is the one who asks permission to sift/tempt Peter. His work runs throughout Scripture and will continue until the end of time.

Chapter 12
Demons (Nephilim) in the New Testament

(Evidence of the fallen lineage operating under the guise of possession and disease)

12.1 Named Demons/Spirits Legion

*References: Markos (Mark) 5:1–20; Lukas (Luke) 8:26–39;
Mattithyahu (Matthew) 8:28–34*

Description: A multitude of demons possessing a man among the Gadarenes. They identify themselves: "Legion, for we are many." They begged Yahusha not to be sent out of the region and entered a herd of swine.

Beelzebul (Beelzebub)

References: Mattithyahu 12:24; Markos 3:22; Lukas 11:15

Description: Called the "prince of demons." The Pârâsh (Pharisees) accused Yahusha of casting out demons by Beelzebul. Related to Baal-Zebub, the Philistine god of Eqrón (2 Kings 1:2).

Satan / Adversary / the Devil (Mastemah)

References: Mattithyahu 4:1–11; Lukas 4:1–13; Yôchânân (John) 8:44; Apokálypsis (Revelation) 12:9

Description: The adversary and accuser; tempter and prince of the fallen messengers. He tempts Yahusha and opposes the truth of the Kingdom.

12.1.2 Types of Evil Spirits

Unclean Spirits

References: Markos 1:23–27; Lukas 4:33–36

Description: General term for demons that possess or torment people. Yahusha expels them with authority.

Deaf and Mute Spirit

References: Markos 9:17–29

Description: Causes muteness, deafness, and convulsions. Yahusha rebukes it: "You deaf and mute spirit, come out of him."

Spirit of Infirmity

References: Lukas 13:11–13

Description: A woman bent over for eighteen years is freed by Yahusha from a spirit of infirmity.

Spirit of Divination (Python)

References: Prásso (Acts) 16:16–18

Description: A servant girl possessed by a spirit of divination who brought profit to her masters. Shaul (Paul) cast it out in the Name of Yahusha Ha Mashiyach.

Spirit of Error / Anti-Mashiyah

References: 1 Yôchânân (1 John) 4:1–6

Description: A spirit that denies Yahusha is the Mashiyach and promotes false teachings.

Spirit of Fear

References: 2 Timotheos 1:7

Description: A demonic influence producing fear and cowardice; contrasted with the ruach of power, love, and self-control.

Spirit of Deception and Fornication

References: Efésios (Ephesians) 2:2; 1 Timotheos 4:1–2; Apokálypsis (Revelation) 18:2

Description: The spirit at work in the sons of disobedience, leading to idolatry, immorality, and spiritual corruption.

12.1.3 Collective or Symbolic Spirits

Seven More Wicked Spirits

References: Mattithyahu 12:43–45; Lukas 11:24–26

Description: When an unclean spirit goes out but finds no rest, it returns with seven worse, symbolizing relapse into greater evil.

Apollyon / Abaddon

References: Apokálypsis (Revelation) 9:11

Legion — Multitude of demons in one man.

References: Markos 5:9 (cf. 5:1–20; Lukas 8:26–39; Mattithyahu 8:28–34).

Beelzebul (Beelzebub) — Prince of demons.

References: Mattithyahu 12:24 (cf. Markos 3:22; Lukas 11:15).

Satan / Devil — Adversary, tempter, accuser.

References: Mattithyahu 4:1–11
(cf. Lukas 4:1–13; Yôchânân 8:44; Apokálypsis 12:9).

Unclean Spirits — Demonic entities in general.

References: Markos 1:23–27 (cf. Lukas 4:33–36).

Deaf & Mute Spirit — Causes muteness and deafness (with convulsions).

References: Markos 9:17–29.

Spirit of Infirmity — Causes physical deformity or affliction.

References: Lukas 13:11–13.

Spirit of Divination (Python) — Deception and fortune-telling.

References: Prásso 16:16–18.

Spirit of Error / Anti-Mashiyah — Promotes false doctrines; denies Yahusha as Mashiyach.

References: 1 Yôchânân 4:1–6.

Spirit of Fear — Produces fear and anxiety; opposed to the ruach of power, love, and self-control.

References: 2 Timotheos 1:7.

Description: The "Destroyer," king over the abyssal demons; ruler of the infernal locusts.

12.1.4 Summary

Seven Worse Spirits — Symbolizes relapse into greater evil after temporary deliverance.

References: Mattithyahu 12:43–45 (cf. Lukas 11:24–26).

Apollyon / Abaddon — Destroyer from the abyss; ruler of abyssal demons.

References: Apokálypsis 9:11.

12.2 Idols and Pagan Deities in the New Testament

(The pagan heritage that infiltrated the New Covenant)

12.2.1 Named Pagan Deities

Artemis (Diana) — Greek goddess (nephilim demon) of fertility and the moon; worshiped in Ephesus. Her temple was one of the Seven "Wonders" of the ancient world.

References: Prásso 19:23–41.

Zeus (Jupiter) — Chief Olympian god (nephilim demon). After a healing in Lystra, the crowd thought Bar-Nabah (Barnabas) was Zeus.

References: Prásso 14:11–13.

Hermes (Mercury) — Greek messenger god (nephilim demon). The people of Lystra identified Shaul as Hermes because he was the chief speaker.

References: Prásso 14:11–13.

Castor and Pollux (Dioscuri) — Twin sons of Zeus; patrons of sailors (Roman nephilim cult). The Alexandrian ship carrying Shaul bore their figurehead ("the Twins").

References: Prásso 28:11.

12.2.2 False Gods and Idols Mentioned Indirectly

"Unknown God" — Athenian altar to an unnamed deity; used by Shaul to proclaim Yahuah, Creator of shâmayim and earth.

References: Prásso 17:22–23.

Baal and Ashtoreth — False gods behind Yâshârêl's apostasies; cited by Shaul referencing the remnant who did not bow to Baal.

References: Rómĕos 11:4 (cf. 1 Melakim 19:18).

Mammon (mammōnas) — Personified deity of wealth; set in opposition to serving Yahuah.

References: Mattithyahu 6:24; Lukas 16:13.

Beelzebul (Beelzebub) — Derived from Baal-Zebub of Eqrón; called "prince of demons" in the NT.

References: Mattithyahu 12:24 (cf. Markos 3:22; Lukas 11:15).

12.2.3 Idolatry and Pagan Cults Condemned

Man-Made Idols — Lifeless works of gold, silver, stone, or wood; condemned throughout Scripture. Revelation warns that humanity "did not repent of worshiping demons and idols."

References: Prásso 17:29; Rómĕos 1:23; Apokálypsis 9:20.

Images of Men, Birds, and Beasts — Humanity exchanged the esteem due to Yahuah for images of creation. Shaul condemns this corruption of worship.

References: Rómĕos 1:23.

The Beast and Its Image — Symbol of end-time idolatry and worship of worldly power under satanic influence; those who worship it are condemned.

References: Apokálypsis 13:14–15; 14:9–11; 19:20.

Babylon the Great (pretended Queen of Heaven) — Global idolatry system/false religion; the harlot who embodies spiritual fornication and the resurgence of ancient goddess cults (Ishtar, Astarte, and others) in rebellion against Yahuah.

References: Apokálypsis 17–18.

12.2.4 Summary

• Artemis (Diana)
Greek; goddess (nephilim demon) of fertility and the moon, worshiped in Ephesus.
References: Prásso 19:23–41.

• Zeus (Jupiter)
Greek; chief Olympian god (nephilim demon).
References: Prásso 14:11–13.

• Hermes (Mercury)
Greek; messenger of the gods (nephilim).
References: Prásso 14:11–13.

• Castor & Pollux (Dioscuri)
Greek/Roman; twin sons of Zeus, sailors' patrons.
References: Prásso 28:11.

- **"Unknown God"**
Greek; Athenian altar to an unnamed deity.
References: Prásso 17:22–23.

- **Baal / Ashtoreth**
Canaanite; false gods of Yâshârêl's apostasy.
References: Rómĕos 11:4.

- **Mammon (mammōnas)**
Aramaic; personified deity of wealth.
References: Mattithyahu 6:24; Lukas 16:13.

- **Beelzebul (Beelzebub)**
Philistine; "lord of the flies," prince of demons.
References: Mattithyahu 12:24.

- **Gold & Silver Idols**
Pagan nations; lifeless objects of worship.
References: Prásso 17:29; Apokálypsis 9:20.

- **Image of the Beast**
Symbolic/Prophetic; idolatry of worldly power.
References: Apokálypsis 13:14–15; 14:9–11; 19:20.

- **Babylon the Great**
Symbolic; world system of false religion and spiritual corruption.
References: Apokálypsis 17–18.

Chapter 13
The Legacy of Constantine

(The Babylonian heritage of the Roman Empire)

13.1 From Babel to Rome: The continuity of pagan worship under a new face

In the time of Emperor Constantine, we clearly see the remnant of the Nephilim and their influence, for he inherited all the teachings and beliefs of Babel.

This remnant also appears in the New Testament—implicitly—through the actions of the Pharisees, when Yahusha Himself called them directly the sons of demons (Nephilim) by saying: "Children of Echidna."

So much so that Yahusha explicitly reveals who their father is—and it is not Yahuah—though many fail to understand this statement.

From the days of Yahusha until today, the world has remained full of the Nephilim remnant, infiltrated into every place, group, and family.

Their favorite activity throughout history has been murdering those who proclaim the words of Yahuah—beginning with the prophets, then Yahusha Himself, and later His disciples and apostles.

13.2 The Creation of the God of the Roman Empire

(The falsification of the divine names and manipulation of the Scriptures)

To consolidate their deception, the Nephilim remnant in Rome carried out a systematic plan:

1. They inserted two letters into the alphabet (J and V) to justify the pagan names "Jehovah" and "Jesus."

2.They erased all the names of Yahuah / Yahusha from the Scriptures in every translation—though in the original Hebrew, these names can never be altered.

3.They leavened the Scriptures with pagan teachings such as the cross, Christian, Christ, and birthdays.

4.They added false sections to justify Nephilim doctrines (such as the Trinity).

5.They conquered nations and rebuilt them from scratch under their new religion and their new god.

6.They created the so-called "canon"—a list of books they permitted humanity to read—while hiding the true canon guarded by the priestly descendants of Aharon in Qumran.

7.They concealed inspired writings, manipulating the term "apocrypha" to make it sound evil or forbidden, when in truth these were the very texts they chose to hide.

8.They invented terms and inserted foreign words into Scripture— such as cross (symbol of the demon Tammuz), Trinity, Christ, Christian, God, Lord, Jesus, Jehovah, and others.

9.They merged pagan feasts, particularly Saturnalia and Christmas, which were celebrated for two main reasons:

- In honor of Saturn, god of agriculture.

- As a tribute to the victory of a conquering general (festival of triumph).

13.3 Saturnalia and "Christmas"

(From sacrifice to Saturn to the decorated tree: the pagan transformation that survived through time)

(Saturnalia, in honor of Saturn, was introduced around 217 B.C. to lift the spirits of Roman citizens after a military defeat by the Carthaginians at Lake Trasimene.

Officially, it was held on December 17, the day of the dedication of Saturn's temple in the Roman Forum, marked by sacrifices, feasts (lectisternium), and the loud public cry "Io Saturnalia!"

The people loved it so much that it was unofficially celebrated for seven days, from December 17 to 23, filled with noisy amusements, orgies, feasting, and the exchange of gifts.

The festivities began with a sacrifice at the temple of Saturn—once the most important deity to Romans before Jupiter—at the foot of the Capitol Hill, followed by a public banquet open to all.

Romans associated Saturn, the agricultural protector of crops and guarantor of harvests, with the pre-Hellenic god Cronos, who ruled during the mythical "Golden Age," when mankind lived happily without social divisions.

During Saturnalia, slaves were often released from their duties and even exchanged roles with their masters.

Over time, "Christmas" was instituted to replace this celebration of Saturn, the king of the sun—where the English word sun became confused with son, making it appear to represent the birth of the "Son of God.")

13.4 December 24 – Eve of Sol Invictus (Christmas)

(The pagan celebration that marked the birth of religious deception)

(On the eve of December 25 in ancient Rome, families gathered and visited one another in preparation for the coming feast—the winter solstice, marking the rebirth of the sun.

Although Saturnalia, in honor of Saturn, was mainly celebrated from December 17 to 23, the eve of Sol Invictus on December 24 was also a day of social and family rejoicing.)

13.5 Birth of Sol Invictus – December 25

(The day Rome exalted the sun-god as the false Messiah of the world)

(Sol Invictus ("Unconquered Sun") was a religious cult of the solar deity that arose in the late Roman Empire.

By the 4th century A.D., the festival of the birth of the Unconquered Sun (Dies Natalis Solis Invicti) celebrated the victory of light over darkness.

After the winter solstice (December 25 in the Julian calendar), the days grew longer—symbolizing the rebirth of the sun.

This same date was already celebrated in Rome as the birthday of the Sun, associated with the god Apollo, another solar deity.

Thus, the Roman world declared December 25 as the "holy day" of the new, imperialized sun-god—later rebranded as the birth of the so-called "Christ.")

13.6 Changing the Shabbath to Sunday

(How imperial power replaced the Creator's rest with the worship of the sun)

(On March 7, 321 A.D., Emperor Constantine I the Great decreed that Sunday, the "venerable day of the Sun"—later renamed by the Catholic Church as "the Lord's Day"—should be observed as a day of rest for judges, the people, and tradesmen, while farmers were permitted to continue working.

This imperial decree formally replaced the divine Shabbath with a solar day of rest, honoring the sun-god rather than Yahuah's sanctified seventh day.)

13.7 Changing the Names of Days and Months

(The manipulation of the divine calendar to impose pagan worship)

The Romans changed the names of the days of the week and months of the year, replacing them with those of pagan gods and demons—just as humanity knows them today.

Originally, the days were numbered simply as first day, second day, and so forth, much like modern Portuguese still preserves (primeiro dia, segundo dia).

The only named day was Shabbath, meaning rest.

In like manner, the months were renamed to honor demons, pagan deities (Nephilim), or men who followed them—completely erasing the divine order of Yahuah's calendar.

13.8 Substitution of the Biblical Feasts

(The replacement of the sacred calendar with pagan celebrations disguised as faith)

All the biblical feasts were forgotten and abolished, replaced by pagan or demonic festivals.

Through this manipulation, the Roman system created holidays for every type of demon or false deity, separating humanity entirely from anything connected with Yahuah.

(Tertullian wrote: "For us, to whom Sabbaths are foreign, and the New Moons and festivals once beloved by God, the Saturnalia, the New Year's festivities, the Winter Solstice, and the Matronalia are now frequented.

Gifts go to and fro; New Year presents are made; games join their noise; banquets join their uproar.

Oh, better fidelity of the nations to their own sect, which does not claim for itself the solemnity of the Christians!

Neither the Day of the Lord nor Pentecost, even if they had known them, would they have shared with us; for they would fear to appear as Christians."

(Tertullian – On Idolatry))

Chapter 14
Babel in the Book of Apokálypsis

(What began with a tower ends with a throne...
the culmination of the ancestral deception)

14.1 The final unveiling of the Babylonian system masked as religion and power

Some still do not grasp the magnitude of how evil has woven itself into everything around us—embraced by the world as if it were "god," blinding many unto the end.

And if we remain unbelieving and deny the facts presented here—and the spread of the Nephilim throughout every sphere—let us see how the last book of the Scriptures devotes many verses and even whole chapters to the Nephilim at the end of days: the reason judgment is coming upon the Nephilim and their descendants, and eternal salvation upon the followers of Yahuah–Yahusha.

Apokálypsis (Revelation) 14:8:
"And there followed another angel, saying, Bâbel is fallen, is fallen, that great city, because she made all nations drink of the wine of the wrath of her pornia."

Pornía: prostitution with other gods (including adultery and incest), idolatry, fornication.

Apokálypsis (Revelation) 16:19:
"And the great city was divided into three parts, and the cities of the nations fell: and great Bâbel came in remembrance before Êlôhîym, to give unto her the cup of the wine of the indignation of his wrath."

Apokálypsis (Revelation) 17:1–2:
"And there came one of the seven angels who had the seven cups, and talked with me, saying unto me, come here; I will show unto you the judgment of the great idolater that sits upon many waters: With whom the kings of the earth have practised idolatry, and the inhabitants of the earth have been made drunk with the wine of her pornia."

Apokálypsis (Revelation) 17:5:
"And upon her forehead was a name written, Mystery, Bâbel the Great, the Mother Of porni and idolatry Of the Earth."

Apokálypsis (Revelation) 17:6:
"And I saw the woman drunken with the blood of the saints, and with the blood of the martyrs of Yahusha: and when I saw her, I wondered with great admiration."

Apokálypsis (Revelation) 17:18:
"And the woman that you saw is that great city (babel), which reigns over the kings of the earth. "

Apokálypsis (Revelation) 18:2:
"And he cried mightily with a strong voice, saying, Bâbel the great is fallen, is fallen, and is become the habitation of demon, and the hold of every unclean spirit, and a cage of every unclean and hateful bird."

Apokálypsis (Revelation) 18:3:
"For all nations have drunk of the wine of the wrath of her pornia, and the kings of the earth have practiced idolatry with

her, and the merchants of the earth are waxed rich through the abundance of her delicacies."

Apokálypsis (Revelation) 18:10:
"Standing afar off for the fear of her torment, saying, woe, woe that great city Bâbel, that mighty city! For in one hour is your judgment come."

Apokálypsis (Revelation) 18:21 & 23:
"And a mighty angel took up a stone like a great millstone, and cast it into the sea, saying, thus with violence shall that great city Bâbel be thrown down, and shall be found no more at all. And the light of a candle shall shine no more at all in you; and the voice of the bridegroom and of the bride shall be heard no more at all in you: for your merchants were the great men of the earth; for by your farmakía were all nations deceived."

Φαρμακεία (farmakía): drugging/"pharmacy," i.e., by extension sorcery, witchcraft (magic, literal or figurative).

Apokálypsis (Revelation) 18:24:
"And in her (bâbel) was found the blood of prophets, and of saints, and of all that were killed upon the earth."

Apokálypsis (Revelation) 19:2:
" For true and righteous are his judgments: for he has judged the great porni, who did corrupt the earth with her pornia, and has avenged the blood of his slaves at her hand. "

Pornia (πορνεία): harlotry, adultery and incest, idolatry, fornication.

If these Scriptures do not at least prompt a reflective pause—to see differently what we think we know—then we will remain in blindness. Yet never forget that only those to whom Yahuah opens their understanding will be able to comprehend the words of this book and receive them as they are.

14.2 The Strategy of the Nephilim Remnant

(Religious infiltration and global spiritual deception)

The strategy has been simple—yet devastatingly effective.

Galátis (Galatians) 2:4:
"And that because of false brethren unawares brought in, who came in privily to spy out our freedom which we have in Mâshiyach Yahusha, to enslave us:"

Yahûdâh (Jude) 1:4:
"For there are certain men crept in unawares, who were before of old ordained to this condemnation, wicked men, turning the grace of our Êlôhîym into lasciviousness, and denying the only Yahuah Êlôhîym, and our Âdônây Yahusha Mâshiyach."

They infiltrate congregations that serve Yahuah, pretending to be devout while not being so.

They take true teachings and alter them so people believe their beliefs are founded in Yahuah—while they are actually following teachings of demons.

But do not forget: the remnant of Yahuah—the counted minority—will have their eyes opened. Yahuah will allow them to see and discern the truth.

Evil and the Nephilim remnant continually seek to destroy Yahuah's followers in every age; yet Yahuah has decreed deliverance and salvation through Yahusha.

We resist understanding and choose blindness. Babel and the Nephilim caused the first destruction of the earth—and they will also be the cause of the last.

It was not—and will not be—the humans who bear the ruach of Yahuah, but the Nephilim lineage that fills the earth and will finally be revealed for what it is.

Have you considered why Yahusha called the Pharisees and Sadducees "Generation of Echidna"?

It means generation of demons, a name linked to the Greek figure of the same term. All this has been hidden so we would not understand the truth.

14.4 The destruction of humanity

(The prophesied fire to consume the works of the Nephilim)

We know the earth will be destroyed once more—but this time by fire.

Recall: the first destruction was by water, and it happened because of the Nephilim, not because of humans. Yahuah saved the only good that remained of His creation: Nôach and his household.

We seldom pause to consider that the reason humanity will be destroyed again is the same as before: the cause of the Nephilim.

It will not be the fault of humans created with the ruach of Yahuah, but of those who carry the remnant, the DNA—the gene—of the Nephilim, continuing to populate and contaminate creation.

Thus, the earth will be destroyed once more—this time, definitively.

14.5 The end mirrors the beginning

(A return to the days of Nôach before the final judgment)

I n the end, the story and the situation are the same—only the times are different.

Evil, intertwined with the blood of the Nephilim remnant, continues to devour and corrupt Yahuah's creation—equal to or worse than in the days of Nôach.

Therefore, we are returning to the days of Nôach—and then the end will come. But this end will be because of the Nephilim.

Yahusha will come to rescue the children of Yahuah—those who bear the chip/gene/DNA of the ruach of Yahuah—before the Nephilim remnant utterly destroys us.

Mattithyâhû (Matthew) 24:37–39:
"But as were the days of Nôach, so shall also be at he coming of the son of man. For as in the days that were before the flood they were eating and drinking, marrying and giving in wedding, until the day that Nôach entered into the ark, And did not know until the flood came, and took them all away; so shall also the coming of the son of man be."

14.6 The final hope

(The rescue of Yahuah's faithful remnant)

The descendants—the chip, the DNA of the Nephilim—are among us.

T hey fill the earth, surround us with their teachings and their offspring, and many times we do not notice.

We keep thinking the guilty ones are the humans who bear the seal of the ruach of Yahuah—unaware that this has been the most skillful lie of all time, crafted to keep us distracted and to prevent us from perceiving the truth.

In this way, they strive to achieve their goal: to drag and corrupt

Yahuah's creation at every moment. They are wholly evil, and their only purpose is to lead Yahuah's creation to perdition.

But we must not fear, for though they try to dress as sheep, they will ever be ravenous wolves; though they present themselves as messengers of light, their deeds reveal who they really are.

To us—the pure, who bear the spiritual DNA of Yahuah—wisdom, understanding, and knowledge have been given to recognize the children of the Nephilim.

Thus we end up separating ourselves from the world entirely: we are in it, but we know it is not our dwelling.

We will dwell with our Yahuah Êlôhîym, and with Yahusha Ha Mashiyach, our eternal King.

Therefore, darkness shall not overcome us.

Though the evil and teachings of the Nephilim—the children of darkness—surround us, we will never be overcome. Light will triumph over darkness.

We will be rescued—and they will be utterly exterminated—this time for all eternity.

Fílippi (Philippians) 2:9–11:
"Therefore Êlôhîym also has highly exalted him, and given him a name which is above every name: That at the name of Yahusha every knee should bow, of things in heaven, and things in earth, and things under the earth; And that every tongue should confess that Yahusha Mâshîyach is Âdônây, to the glory of Êlôhîym the father."

1 Thessalonikéfs (1 Thessalonians) 4:16–17:
"For Âdônây himself shall descend from heaven with a shout, with the voice of the archangel, and with the trump of Êlôhîym:

and the dead in Mâshıyach shall rise first: Then we which are alive and remain shall be caught up together with them in the clouds, to meet Âdônây in the air: and so we shall be always with Âdônây."

Chapter 15
The Origin of Evil and Wickedness

(From the heavenly rebellion to human corruption and extermination)

The summary of the origin of evil and wickedness is not exactly what we have been taught.

This is understandable, because the purpose of the Nephilim lineage—of Babel—is to confuse, and we are easily persuaded by Nephilim lies.

The truth is that the disasters known in human history—often blamed on humans created by Yahuah—are not entirely their doing.

15.1 The end of the Watcher-Nephilim

Although humanity remains hypnotized by the Watchers, their Nephilim descendants, their offspring the demons, and their doctrines of perdition—their destiny is certain, and nothing can change the outcome. That is why they strive to drag along as many as they can.

Chănôk (Enoch) – Chapter 21: Verses 8–10:
"Then I said: How fearful is the place and how terrible to look upon! Then Ûriyêl answered me, one of the qâdôsh angels who was with me, and said unto me: Chănôk, why you have such fear and affright? And I answered: Because of this fearful place, and because of the spectacle of the pain. And he said unto me: This place is the prison of the angels, and here they will be imprisoned forever."

Chănôk (Enoch) – Chapter 54: Verse 6:
"And Mıykâêl, and Gabrıyêl, and Râphâêl, and Phanuêl shall take hold of them on that great day, and cast them on that day into the burning furnace, that Yahuah of Rûach may take vengeance on them for their unrighteousness in becoming subject to the adversary and leading astray those who dwell on the earth."

Yôbêl (Jubilees) – Chapter 5: Verse 6:
"And against the angels whom he had sent upon the earth, he was exceedingly wroth, and he gave commandment to root them out of all their dominion, and he bid us to bind them in the depths of the earth, and behold they are bound in the midst of them, and are kept separate."

Yôbêl (Jubilees) – Chapter 5: Verse 10:
"And their fathers were witnesses of their destruction, and after this they were bound in the depths of the earth forever, until the day of the great condemnation, when judgment is executed on all those who have corrupted their ways and their works before Yahuah."

The final fate of the Watchers was sealed from the moment they sinned. They were confined in dark prisons, awaiting the day of final judgment when they will be tormented forever.

Mattithyâhû (Matthew) – Chapter 13: Verses 41–42:
"The son of man shall send forth his angels, and they shall gather
out of his kingdom all things that causes evil, and them that do
iniquity; And shall cast them into a furnace of fire: there shall be
wailing and gnashing of teeth."

15.2 The Origin and the End of Evil

(The complete story of deception and final redemption)

15.2.1 The Fall in the Beginning

• Gadreel seduces Chawwâh (Eve) into sin.

In the Yarden, Gadreel—one of the celestial beings appointed as a guardian—deceived Chawwâh to eat the forbidden fruit. Thus sin entered creation, corrupting human purity and opening the door to spiritual deception (Berēshīth 3:1–6).

• Only humans can procreate with the spirit of Yahuah.

Yahuah's design was that only humans, made in His image,
would bear His ruach. Celestial beings were not created to mix
with mortal flesh (Berēshīth 1:27–28).

15.2.2 The Rebellion of the Watchers

• The Watcher angels descend and change their purpose to create offspring.

In the days before the flood, the Watchers descended upon Mount
Hermon to beget children with the daughters of men
(Chănôk/Enoch 6:1–6).

• The Watchers were themselves seduced and deceived.

These beings were manipulated by spirits of rebellion with promises of power and rule on earth.

- The children of the Watchers and women do not have the spirit of Yahuah.

This unnatural union produced the Nephilim—giants bereft of the divine breath. They were not created by Yahuah's breath but by a mixture of flesh and corrupted celestial power (Berēshīth 6:4).

- Demons were the product of the union of women with the Watchers.

When the Nephilim died in the flood, their spirits remained earthbound, without bodies or rest. These are the demons who seek to inhabit human bodies (Chănôk 15:8–10).

- Demons were created by humans (women) and the Watchers.

They are not Yahuah's work but the fruit of corruption and rebellion; therefore they are condemned until the final judgment (Chănôk 16:1–3).

15.2.3 The Flood and the Purification of the Earth

- The flood came because of the sin of the Nephilim.

The earth was filled with violence and corruption. Yahuah determined to destroy all flesh contaminated by the seed of the Watchers (Berēshīth 6:11–13).

- The flood was sent to save the eight humans who had the spirit of Yahuah.

Nôach and his family alone preserved genetic and spiritual purity; through them humanity was preserved (Berēshīth 7:1).

- The Nephilim perished in the flood and became demons.

Their bodies were destroyed, but their spirits remained

wandering, seeking rest and causing oppression (Chănôk 15:9–12).

• Yahuah covenanted not to destroy the earth again by water.

After the flood, Yahuah established His covenant with Nôach, sealed by the rainbow as a sign of mercy (Berēshĭth 9:11–13).

15.2.4 The Return of Deception after the Flood

• A Nephilim family escaped and survived the flood.

According to ancient traditions, a small contaminated remnant remained and, after the flood, sheltered in the mountains of Ararat (Turkey).

• The remnant ran aground on Ararat and settled in Babel.

There they began to rebuild their dominion, guided by the forbidden teachings of the Watchers.

• Qeynan found the teachings of the Watchers, copied them, and taught them.

Qeynan, a descendant of Nôach, discovered the hidden writings of the Watchers, reintroducing sorcery, astrology, and corrupt arts (Jubilees 8:1–4).

• The teachings of the Watchers are the root of all destruction.

From them sprang occult practices, false cults, and sciences that again corrupted the nations.

15.2.5 Babel and the Spread of Evil

• The Watchers (or their remnant) inhabited Babel.

The civilization of Nimrod and Babel revived the ancient heavenly rebellion, seeking to reach the heavens by forbidden power (Berēshīṯh 11:1–4).

- Construction of the Tower of Babel.

It represented a human–demonic attempt to reunite heaven and earth under a single corrupted rule.

- Yahuah confuses the languages and disperses the Nephilim remnant.

To halt evil's spread, Yahuah confused their speech and scattered the nations (Berēshīṯh 11:7–9).

- The Nephilim remnant spread among all nations.

Their tainted lineages infiltrated many peoples, carrying idolatry, human sacrifice, and false gods.

- The remnant conquered Sodom, Gomorrah, and the neighboring cities.

These cities became centers of Nephilim perversion, where mixture and sin peaked (Berēshīṯh 19).

- Sodom and Gomorrah were destroyed for the sin of the Nephilim.

Fire and sulfur descended from shâmayim as Yahuah's judgment upon their genetic and spiritual corruption.

15.2.6 The Rule of Evil in Yâshârêl and the Ancient World

- The Nephilim gave rise to the Chasmoniym, fathers of the Philistines.

From them came warlike peoples and enemies of Yahuah's people, whose idolatry filled the land with blood.

- Pharisees, Sadducees, and Essenes are Hasmonean (Nephilim) descendants.

These religious factions dominated the Second-Temple era, corrupting Torâh with human traditions.

• The Samaritans usurped the temple and changed the high priest.

After the kingdom's division, the Samaritans adopted their own sacred mountain and a false priesthood (Yôchânân 4:20–22).

• Maśṭêmâh was appointed over the demons, head of the Nephilim remnant.

Designated prince of evil spirits, he coordinates the spiritual rebellion against the chosen (Jubilees 10:8–9).

• Maśṭêmâh is not a demon but a physical messenger, with a body.

Unlike unclean spirits, Maśṭêmâh has bodily form and can manifest in only one place at a time.

• Maśṭêmâh and Asmodeus dwelt in Mitsrayim (Egypt).

Egypt served as their power center, influencing kings, magicians, and priests against Môsheh and the chosen people.

15.2.7 The Manifestation of Yahusha and the Final Redemption

• Yahusha confronts Nephilim groups (Pharisees, Sadducees, Essenes).

During His ministry, Yahusha exposed the religious elites preserving the blood and teachings of Babel:

"You are of your father, the diábolos..." (Yôchânân 8:44).

• Pharisees, Sadducees, and Essenes kill Yahusha and persecute His disciples.

Thus the ancient enmity between the seed of the woman and the seed of the serpent was fulfilled (Berēshīth 3:15).

• Babel is the cradle of the Nephilim remnant.

From antiquity, Babel represents the spiritual system of evil—the root of all idolatry and false religion (Apokálypsis 17:5).

• Constantine adopts the teachings of the Nephilim and of Babel.

His imperial religion mixed the faith with Babylonian practices; his household carried Babylonian lineage, reinforcing a politico-religious union.

• Today's religious leaders are part of the Wicked Priest's line.

From the same Nephilim lines arose modern ecclesiastical systems—heirs of Babylonian corruption.

• The religion created by Constantine is the religion of Babel.

It replaced the sacred Names, imposed idols, and established Rome's spiritual dominion over the nations.

• The religion of the Roman Empire became the new cradle of Babel.

Rome perpetuated the Watchers' work—melding politics, idolatry, and global spiritual control.

• Babel again devours humanity and drives it to destruction.

The same spirit of rebellion dominates the religious, economic, and cultural systems of the present world.

• Humanity's destruction comes again through the sin of Babel and the Nephilim.

• 2 Kêph (2 Peter) - Chapter-3: Verse-7:

• "But the heavens and the earth, which are now, by the same word are kept in store, reserved unto fire against the Day of Judgment and perdition of wicked men."

• Yahuah–Yahusha will rescue His people and restore creation.

The chosen will be delivered from Babel's corruption and will live with Him forever, as planned from the beginning (Apokálypsis 21:3–4).

Conclusion
From Rebellion to Redemption

(The invisible story of evil comes to an end... and the glory of Elyôn shines forever.)

The history of evil is, in reality, the history of deception. From Gadreel to Maśṭêmâh, from Babel to Rome, the same Nephilim roots have manifested under different names, religions, and powers. Yet the eternal purpose of Yahuah has never changed: to rescue His creation and establish His eternal Kingdom in righteousness.

The Watchers and their offspring sowed corruption, but Yahuah raised up Yahusha ha Mashiyach to restore what was lost. "For the Son of Man came to seek and to save what was lost" (Lukas / Luke 19:10). By His death and resurrection, Yahusha broke the chain of the Nephilim, disarmed principalities and powers, and triumphed over them publicly. "And having disarmed principalities and powers, he made a show of them openly, triumphing over them in it." (Kolosse / Colossians 2:15).

The enemy attempted to perpetuate his lineage through empires, religion, and political power, but his entire system is destined to fall. "Fallen, fallen is Babylon the Great, and she has become a habitation of demons..." (Apokálypsis / Revelation 18:2). Thus the destiny will be fulfilled for all who rejected the ruach of Yahuah and followed the teachings of the Watchers.

But those who remain in Yahusha will be delivered. They will inherit the promised Kingdom, where there will be no corruption, no mixture, no death. "Then I saw a new shâmayim and a new earth... and there shall be no more death, nor mourning, nor crying, nor pain..." (Apokálypsis / Revelation 21:1–4).

The beginning of evil started with a forbidden mixture; its end will be total purification. The plan of Yahuah has always been to redeem, restore, and dwell with His people. "And I heard a great voice from shâmayim saying, 'Behold, the tabernacle of Êlôhîym is with men, and He will dwell with them; and they shall be His people, and Êlôhîym Himself will be with them and be their Êlôhîym.'" (Apokálypsis / Revelation 21:3).

Thus the account comes to its conclusion: evil had its origin, its expansion, and its dominion; but it will also have its end. Babel will fall, the Watchers will be judged and tormented eternally, the Nephilim and the demons exterminated. Then Yahusha, the Mashiyach, will reign over all the earth. And the redeemed will live in eternity as Yahuah planned from the beginning: in purity, truth, and eternal love.

Apokálypsis (Revelation) 20:8–10
"And he will go out to deceive the nations which are in the four corners of the earth, Gôg and Mâgôg, to gather them together to battle; the number of whom is as the sand of the sea. And they went up over the breadth of the earth and surrounded the camp of the Qâdôsh and the beloved city; and fire came down from shâmayim from Êlôhîym and consumed them. And the diábolos who deceived them was cast into the lake of fire and sulfur, where the beast and the false prophet are, and they will be tormented day and night forever and ever."

This is the clear, precise, concise, and exact end of the evil that has scourged the human race since ancient days. Here all rebellion ends, all corruption ends, all dominion of darkness ends.

The adversary—after being released for a short time—goes out again to deceive the demonic (Nephilim) nations, gathering all his henchmen: the Nephilim remnant and the demonic spirits who were imprisoned since the Flood—innumerable, like the sand of the sea.

This is his final desperate attempt, his last act of rebellion. Together they surround the camp of the Qâdôsh (the saints) and the beloved city, the New Yarushaláyim, where we dwell—those redeemed and sealed in Yahusha Ha Mashiyach.

• But there is no battle.

• There is no war.

• No confrontation is even possible.

The power of Elyôn requires neither swords nor armies: fire descends from shâmayim from Êlôhîym, and in an instant it consumes all evil spirits. Their corruption devours them from within; their own fallen nature is their eternal condemnation.

These demons—born of the forbidden union between the Watcher messengers and the daughters of men—were created in corruption, and therefore are completely exterminated.

There is no return, no second chance—this is the absolute end of evil, the second death finally consummated and complete. End of the story.

Only those eternal and immortal beings who sinned—the rebellious messengers, the adversary himself, Mastemá, Gadreel, together with the beast and the false prophet—are not consumed, but tormented forever and ever in the lake of fire and sulfur, prepared for them from the beginning.

These are they who, being eternal, sinned in their eternity—and in that same eternity will endure eternal judgment.

• Thus all justice is fulfilled.

• Thus the divine sentence is sealed.

• Thus the dominion of evil ends, and the eternal, glorious Kingdom of the Mashiyach rises. Yahuah, our Êlôhîym, will reign forever, and His light will guide the redeemed for all eternity.

END OF THE STORY.

THE CURTAIN ON EVIL HAS FALLEN.

ALL THINGS BEGIN AND END IN YAHUAH. HE IS OUR PURPOSE, PEACE AND ETERNITY.

Bibliography

Mason, Kenneth. *The Himalayan Journal* — "The Passing of Mummery." 1931, pp. 11, 14, and 15.

Used as historical context on early Himalayan explorations and their symbolic parallel to humanity's spiritual quest.

Advantour. *"Armenia: Geography."* https://www.advantour.com/es/armenia/geografia.htm

Provides geographic and historical information on Armenia and the Ararat region related to Flood accounts.

Advantour. *"Mount Ararat."* https://www.advantour.com/es/armenia/ararat.htm

Reference for the historical/symbolic location of Mount Ararat and its biblical importance in Genesis.

Wikipedia. *"Himalaya."* https://es.wikipedia.org/wiki/Himalaya?variant=zh-cn

Used to establish geographic details of ancient mountains and their relation to divine settings.

Wikipedia. *"Monte Everest."* https://es.wikipedia.org/wiki/Monte_Everest

Detailed article on the world's highest mountain; includes location, ascent history, and symbolism as an extreme point of the ancient world.

Wikipedia. *"Amonitas."* https://es.wikipedia.org/wiki/Amonitas

Provides information on biblical nations that opposed Israel, linked to spiritual corruption.

Wikipedia. *"Moabitas."* https://es.wikipedia.org/wiki/Moabitas

Historical and genealogical context on Moab, relevant to lines of ancestral rebellion.

Wikipedia. *"Brujería."* https://es.wikipedia.org/wiki/Brujer%C3%ADa

Explains ancient practices and their spiritual parallels with teachings of the fallen Watchers.

Wikipedia. *"Magia."* https://es.wikipedia.org/wiki/Magia

Clarifies ancient definitions and rituals of magic across civilizations.

Wikipedia. *"Morcilla."* https://es.wikipedia.org/wiki/Morcilla

Cited for its historical relation to blood practices and cultural parallels.

Univisión. *"Maquillaje letal: productos de belleza que se usaban y podían causar la muerte."* https://www.univision.com/estilo-de-vida/belleza/maquillaje-letal-productos-de-belleza-que-se-usaban-y-podian-causar-la-muerte

Used to illustrate vanity and the dangers of lethal beauty from antiquity to the present.

Vogue México. *"El delineado cat-eye: cuál es su historia."* https://www.vogue.mx/belleza/articulo/delineado-cat-eye-cual-es-su-historia

Source on the historical symbolism of eye makeup in ancient cultures.

GemSelect. *"Significado de las gemas."* https://www.gemselect-spain.com/spanish/other-info/gemstone-meanings.php

Reference on symbolic and occult meanings attributed to precious stones.

Tonello. *"Historia del teñido: de los orígenes a nuestros días."* https://inspiring.tonello.com/es/historia-del-tenido-de-los-origenes-a-nuestros-dias/

Used to analyze cultural symbolism of colors and textiles in ancient religious contexts.

BibleHub. *"Septuagint Genesis 10."* https://biblehub.com/sep/genesis/10.htm

Cited for genealogical comparisons and the dispersion of nations after Babel.

Virtual Religion Network. *"The Habakkuk Dead Sea Scroll (1QpHab)."* https://virtualreligion.net/iho/1QpHab.html

Used to understand prophetic and rebellion themes found at Qumran.

Wikipedia. *"Equidna (Mythology)."* https://es.wikipedia.org/wiki/Equidna_(mitolog%C3%ADa)

Provides mythological context on hybrid creatures symbolizing corruption.

Wikipedia. *"Saturnales."* https://es.wikipedia.org/wiki/Saturnales

Used to show the pagan origin of Roman festivities later adopted by religious institutions.

BBC Mundo. *"El origen del Sol Invictus y las fiestas romanas."* https://www.bbc.com/mundo/noticias-59298500

Basis for analyzing December 25 and its connection to the worship of Sol Invictus.

Wikipedia. *"Sol Invictus."* https://es.wikipedia.org/wiki/Sol_Invictus

Expands details on the Roman cult incorporated into imperial and later traditions.

Wikipedia. *"Sábado."* https://es.wikipedia.org/wiki/S%C3%A1bado

Explains historical changes in Shabbath observance and their theological implications.

El Libro Perdido de Enki.

Used to compare ancient Mesopotamian myths with biblical accounts of creation and rebellion.